At the Feet of a Himalayan Master

At the Feet of a Himalayan Master

Remembering Swami Rama

volume three

Prakash Keshaviah, Ph.D., Editor

Himalayan Institute Hospital Trust
Swami Ram Nagar, P.O. Doiwala
Distt. Dehradun 248140, Uttarakhand, India

Editor: Prakash Keshaviah, Ph.D.

Library of Congress Control Number: 2012913103

ISBN 978-81-88157-69-3

All proceeds from the sale of this book go to benefit Swami Rama Centre.

Published by:

Himalayan Institute Hospital Trust
Swami Ram Nagar, P.O. Doiwala
Distt. Dehradun 248140
Uttarakhand, India
tel: 91-135-247-1233, fax: 91-135-247-1122
src@hihtindia.org, www.hihtindia.org

Available through Swami Rama Centre, HIHT, Swami Ram Nagar, P.O. Doiwala, Distt. Dehradun 248140, Uttarakhand, India. 0135-247-1233, src@hihtindia.org.

Contents

Acknowledgments

It is very fulfilling to bring out Volume 3 of the series *At the Feet of a Himalayan Master: Remembering Swami Rama.* This volume has been possible only because of the generosity of the five contributors, June Gable, Shri Roshan Lal, Dr. Renu Kapoor, Shri K. N. Mehrotra and Dr. Hema De Munnik in sharing their reminiscences with us. We thank them for the time and effort taken in penning their narratives. We are indebted to Kamal Didi (Patrice Hafford) for her painstaking efforts in page layout, cover design and proofreading. This book would not have been possible without her hard work and dedication. We thank Shri Swami Veda Bharatiji who, despite a hectic schedule agreed to write the inspiring Foreword to this book. Last but not least, we would like to thank Parvathy Rangappa for conscientiously proofreading the entire manuscript.

Foreword

The word 'great' is cognate to 'guru,' both derived from the same original verb root. So also the words 'gravity' and 'gravitation.' All those who are initiated into any genuine tradition gravitate towards the great guru.

The greatness of the Guru is in that he, like a mother, gestates us in the womb of his knowledge. The first guru, hiranyagarbha, is the Golden Womb of the universe in that all knowledge dwells in that cosmic womb.

When the Guru takes our foetus-like, undeveloped consciousness, and keeps it in the spacious womb of his own consciousness, thereby we become his offspring.

This relationship in the Tradition is the most sacred. We may pay our debt to our physical parents by honoring and serving them. From the Guru, there is no such expectation because the value of knowledge can never be assessed.

The purpose of this knowledge in the spiritual traditions is simply moksha, liberation. Further, the purpose of passing on the knowledge is for the compassion towards all living beings, to liberate them from their suffering, to provide them with a boat to cross the rivers of sorrow.

Every time we recite the 'tryambakam' mantra, the central prayer in that mantra is a single word

MUKSHEEYA, "May I be liberated." This should be our aspiration and longing day and night, muksheeya!

When we have such aspiration, the Guru himself will gravitate towards us and draw us into the field of his gravity pull. He will keep us there until our wish 'muksheeya' has been fulfilled.

Those who are writing for the series *At the Feet of a Himalayan Master* were either all longing for this spiritual liberation or they were led by the Master, Swami Rama of the Himalayas, to cultivate that longing and make it their long term goal.

This third volume will perform another one of the services that also the previous two volumes have performed. Those who do not understand the Master often have questions about the Master's meanings and motives and the puzzling 'koans' that he often presented to the disciples to resolve the riddles and contradictions of mind and life. The reader will find ample inspiring episodes of these riddles and resolutions remembered by the writers in these volumes.

The volumes need to be read not just as interesting stories about a great man, the likes of whom are born once in many a century, but as inspirations and guidance for life. These should also be read as guidance on the path of liberation.

This valuable work undertaken by the Swami Rama Centre at Himalayan Institute Hospital Trust by Kamal Didi and Dr. Prakash Keshaviah will guide many generations to come on the paths hallowed by the Himalayan masters. These volumes will indeed make us gravitate towards the greatness of the universal Guru Spirit that incarnates in our midst to guide us.

Swami Veda Bharati, Guru Purnima, 3 July 2012

Preface

This is the preface to Volume 3 of the series, *At the Feet of a Himalayan Master: Remembering Swami Rama*. This volume has five contributors: Ms. June Gable, Shri Roshan Lal, Dr. Renu Kapoor, Shri K. N. Mehrotra and Dr. Hema de Munnik. These five contributors are of diverse nationalities and backgrounds, but share a common bond of great reverence and love for Swami Rama as evidenced by their narratives. They approached Swamiji at different times, for different reasons and with different aspirations. Dr. Renu Kapoor was only eight years old when Swamiji graced her home in 1958. Dr. Hema de Munnik did not meet Swamiji till 1991 when she was 54 years old. Despite these differences in age, background, temperament and nationality, they found in Swami Rama a true friend, profound philosopher and compassionate guide.

June Gable is a Tony Award nominated American actress who met Swami Rama in 1983 at the nadir of her theatric career. Being an actress, she hid behind many masks and refused to come to terms with who she really was. Swami Rama's approach to stripping her of these pretentious masks was often painful to June's sensibilities, but in the end, his fatherly love and compassionate guidance led her to self-acceptance, nonattachment, and the ability to make the teachings of yoga an integral part of her life. As Ms. June Gable concludes, "What did I learn? Volumes! Joy, music, focus of energy, direction, silence, discipline, clean living, self-respect, gardening, service, truthfulness, nonattachment, freedom, creativity and acceptance!"

Shri Roshan Lal, a successful businessman of Kanpur, first met Swami Rama in 1948 when he was known as Patti Wale Baba (Leaf Baba) because of his austerities of keeping his arms upraised all the time and surviving on the leaves that hung from the branches of trees. This was even before Swami Rama was anointed as the Shankaracharya of Karvirpitham. After the first meeting, Roshan Lalji could not meet Swami Rama again till 1960, after he had renounced his position as Shankaracharya and was living on the outskirts of Kanpur. Swami Rama immediately recognized that Roshan Lalji craved the love of his mother who had passed away when he was very young. Swamiji declared that from then on, he would be both father and mother to Roshan Lalji. Roshan Lalji had the privilege of Swamiji's love and guidance for more than three decades and was witness not only to the amazing yogic powers of Swamiji but also to revelations of his divinity.

Dr. Renu Kapoor, a lecturer in psychology with a D.Litt. in Indian psychology from Kanpur University, was blessed by Swami Rama in 1958 when she was only eight years old. The whole family was spellbound when a tall, handsome monk with shaven head, clad in saffron robes and holding a staff, entered their home. The young monk, known then as Swami Ram Dandi, was in Kanpur to deliver a series of lectures. He came to their home looking for her father who had been his classmate earlier at Allahabad University. Swamiji's frequent visits to their home made a profound impression on the young Renu. She received from Swamiji the blessings of Saraswathi, the goddess of learning and wisdom and also his guidance in completing her dissertation for her D.Litt. She also received practical lessons in hospitality, aesthetics, relationships and purposeful living. She concludes her narrative with the wo₁ 's, "He was an unfathomable ocean, while I am only ₐ drop."

Shri K. N. Mehrotra has been practicing civil law in Kanpur for four decades. He first met Swami Rama in 1959, when Swamiji was known as Swami Ram Dandi. His next meeting with Swamiji was in 1963, soon after his marriage. Swamiji was in Kanpur and came to bless the young couple. Over the years, Mehrotraji had many occasions to witness Swamiji's mysterious yogic siddhis (powers), his solicitious concern for Mehrotra's family and his humanitarian efforts for the residents of Uttarakhand. As he remarks, "Those who thought of Swamiji as an ordinary human being, experienced immense grief when he departed the body, whereas, those who looked upon him as divine are still getting instructions from him."

Dr. Hema de Munnik, a clinical psychologist and experienced yoga teacher from the Netherlands, first met Swami Rama in 1991 in Curacao at a weekend seminar organized by the Himalayan Institute. She was going through a very difficult period in her life trying to cope with the breakup with her Antillean partner. Her first impression of Swami Rama was not very favorable. Despite this, she journeyed to India with a tour group organized by the Himalayan Institute. During her stay at the Rishikesh ashram, Swamiji shocked her by declaring that he would make her a yoga teacher and help her establish the Himalayan Institute of Curacao. He also instructed her to receive a mantra initiation from him. Perplexed and confused, Hema decided to go with the flow and receive mantra initiation. She had an amazing inner experience when

Swamiji blessed her by touching her forehead after the mantra initiation. This was a significant turning point in her life. Though her physical association with Swamiji lasted only five years, he taught her to face her fears and overcome her inadequacies through determination, introspection and yoga. With his loving support, she became a skilled yoga teacher in the Combined Therapy Program at Honesdale, Pennsylvania and returned to Curacao to help run the newly established Himalayan Institute of Curacao. Hema had the privilege of returning to India towards the end of Swami Rama's earthly life and he helped her deal not only with her sorrow at seeing his disease-ridden body but also taught her to confront death and disease in ways that she had never thought possible.

The cover of this volume shows the youthful Swami Rama, as he must have appeared to Roshan Lalji, Renu Kapoor and Mehrotraji, when he met them in Kanpur in the early 1960s. By including the firsthand experiences of the five contributors to this volume, we hope to present for future generations a true portrait of Swamiji that does not suffer from the distortions of time and clime. As pointed out in the preface to previous volumes of these series, the differences in the narrators and their narratives serve an important purpose—the opportunity to view Swami Rama from many different perspectives from which one can construct for oneself a composite portrait of Swami Rama, the multi-faceted phenomenon who graced our lives.

June Gable

❧

Junie's Song

June Gable

June Gable is an actress who has played varying roles in theatres in New York City, London, and all across America. She was nominated for a Tony Award for her performance in "Candide" and won an Obie Award, for Off-Broadway excellence, in Shakespeare's "A Comedy of Errors." She appeared in many TV comedies in Hollywood over the years, most notably, the NBC series, "Friends." She is a graduate of Carnegie-Mellon University and is also a published writer and painter.

June remains a therapist and a yoga teacher, certified by the Himalayan Institute. She ran the "Little Yoga Studio of Hollywood" for 13 years.

Chapter 1

At the Feet of the Master

Waiting for the word of the Master,
Watching the Hidden Light;
Listening to catch His orders
In the very midst of the fight;

Seeing His slightest signal
Across the heads of the throng;
Hearing His faintest whisper
Above earth's loudest song.

From At the Feet of the Master, *by J. Krishnamurti*

I had been a successful actress with a Tony Award nomination, but I had a history of addictions and had become a feisty alcoholic. In the early part of 1983, my Broadway show had flopped miserably, opening and closing on the same night. I was on the verge of losing everything I owned, my car had broken down, no one returned my phone calls, and every romantic relationship had ended in disaster. I was definitely at a crossroads. As Swami Rama said to me later, "You were lucky everyone spat on you!"

I met Swami Rama for the first time in June of the same year. Several weeks earlier, I had stumbled into the East/West Bookstore, the New York City outlet of the Himalayan International Institute of Yoga Science and Philosophy. Severely inebriated, having just left my ex-boyfriend at the bar, I had stumbled into the bookstore to get out of the pouring rain. I must have looked like a bedraggled, lost puppy, soaking wet and with my black mascara streaming down my face. Everyone in the bookstore was very nice and helpful. They could clearly see that I was a lost, desperate soul in need of some help and guidance. As my clothes dried, they told me about a Swami Rama, the founder of the Himalayan International Institute, and about the upcoming Congress in Honesdale, Pennsylvania. Several of them were going to attend the Congress and asked if I would like to come along.

In Honesdale, I was taken to meet Swami Rama who was surrounded by a coterie of people. I had difficulty looking him, or anybody else for that matter, in the eye. Nobody said anything. I finally looked up. I had never seen anyone so tall, particularly someone from India! The wind whipped around his robes and the sun shone behind his silver hair, like a halo. He had huge dark eyes that seemed to see right through me and he had a big grin on his face.

"So, you are an actress?" he asked.

I was shocked. Who told him?

"Yes Swami," I said, hesitatingly.

"You mean they pay you to do this?" he asked, his voice low and guttural.

I felt intimidated.

"Yes, Swami, I get paid," I said.

There was a pause.

"Why?" he boomed out. "We're all acting!"

Everyone around him just laughed and laughed. Everyone, except me.

A moment passed.

He bent down towards me. I noticed the faint smell of Turkish cigarettes. Ah ha! So he smoked!

"Are you a go-go dancer, or maybe, a doo-doo dancer, eh?"

Everyone laughed again.

What the hell was he talking about?

He continued, "Hunters are not allowed in this ashram. Are you looking for a husband?"

I was not used to this kind of conversation!

"No," I lied (as usual).

"Then, why are you here?" he asked.

I tried to impress him: "Swami, I want to learn yoga. I want my life to be different."

He looked thoughtful. "My schedule is tight right now, I accept only serious sadhakas, serious students."

I became insistent: "Swami, I want to learn renunciation!"

Laughing he said, "Oh no! If you become my first lady swami there will be no more renunciates!"

At that, he turned and walked away, his students following like sheep.

I stood there, completely stunned. I could hear them all laughing as they moved towards the building. I had been dismissed! How infuriating. How dare he? After all, I was almost famous! I started to cry, and turned to walk up a huge hill to my car. It had been a fairly mild, ordinary day. Suddenly, huge black clouds seemed to be coming towards me over the hills. Then, the skies opened up and I was pelted with large hailstones and driving rain, which literally brought me to my knees.

But I knew that no matter what, I would come back to this place, and see this strange man again. My fate was irrevocably sealed that day.

Chapter 2

In retrospect, it seemed propitious that two rainstorms heralded my seeking a new way of life through yoga. I think of the water images in the words of Shri Chaitanya: ". . . . that the mirror of the heart may be wiped clean . . . . stream down, in moonlight, on the lotus-heart . . . . that bath, for weary souls . . . ."

Some weeks after that first meeting with Swami Rama, I had a dream. I wrote about it with passion in my diary. Dreams are sometimes prophetic, sometimes fantasies, born out of fear or desires, conscious or unconscious. But the dream state can be meaningful and important. I had five dreams of Swami Rama, all of them prophetic. This is how I recorded my first dream:

> I knew he was my true friend, because he
>   appeared to me, late one night.
> Tall, so tall, I couldn't even see the top of
>   his head.
> Yet I recognized him! Why was he here,
> Among the shadows on my wall?
> He looked down at me, so I called out;
> Stony, he did not answer.
> I crawled over, and firmly grasped his
>   ankles,
> And he turned into a tree!
> A giant of a tree, a huge Redwood,
>   immobile yet yielding,

He comforted me, while I held on to him
Rooted as he was in the earth.
And I knew he was my eternal friend,
In that he would always guide me,
Sometimes noisy, sometimes silent,
Through my darkest night.

I waxed poetic, I know, and embraced a romantic idea of what it would be like "At the Feet of the Master." I booked a flight to India through the Himalayan Institute. I felt I had to see him again. I had no idea what I was getting myself into!

At the airport, I was met by some people who were part of the same group tour. We were to stay that night at the Hyatt Hotel in New Delhi before proceeding to Swami Rama's Ashram in Rishikesh the next morning. I went straight to the hotel bar and stayed up late drinking with an attractive businessman from Germany. The next day, slightly hung over, I looked out of my window. I saw a beautiful white pigeon which had nested with her baby birds on the window ledge of my hotel room. I did not consider this as particularly meaningful, but later, Swami Rama said that it was an auspicious omen.

When we got to Rishikesh, I noticed people bending down to touch Swami Rama's feet. I went over to him and tried to do the same. He seemed annoyed and moved away. "A stupid custom!" he muttered. "I put up with it here in India, but not everyone should do this!"

There was very little else of a welcome for me. Then, as if to prove a point, he said, "You like shoes so much? I have a job for you right now. See all those shoes?" There were many sneakers and sandals in a clump by the door. "Pick them up," he ordered, "move them to the other end of the building!" My mouth fell open. But I obeyed. Why was I doing this? One

of the Indian ladies at the ashram defended me and
began to remonstrate with Swami Rama. He ignored
her. Everyone went inside to eat lunch, except me, the
shoes and him. He stood there, watching me. Finally,
he told me to stop, wash my hands and come in to eat.

Chapter 3

The incident with the shoes turned out to be the first of many ordeals I was to endure. As time went on, I discovered that in the yoga tradition, there would be times when I would have to do certain things in order to learn more about myself and others. It was a process I didn't always like or understand, but it ultimately made sense, sometimes years later. For an arrogant person like me, to learn humility was to learn truth. Pride and ego had to be destroyed; the heart needed to crack open, hurt and bleed a bit, before the re-building could begin. This was how Swami Rama taught me. He let me figure these things out, but always made sure that I got the point!

Some of the most difficult lessons took place early on. That night, he continued, asking me many questions about my life, in front of the other members of the group. He asked me if I had a dog and what kind it was. I told him that I had a dog that looked like a sheep dog, but it really wasn't. She was a mixed breed.

He responded, "Deceptive, eh? Just like her mom!"

Was he calling me a liar? I knew that I was. I lied often. He seemed to be able to confront me on all levels of self-deception. No one had ever stripped these layers off me before. For example, I had always been deeply ashamed of my background. I came from a family of immigrants.

He questioned me, "Is your mother Jewish?"

"No!" I lied.

Again, he pushed me, "If your mother is Jewish, then you are too!"

How did he know? Who told him? I became angry, defensive. "I'm a Christian!" My voice rose. "I am Irish and Italian!" Couldn't he tell that I was Irish? After all, I had dyed my hair red!

For the next two weeks, he would shout daily:

"Where's the little Jewess?" Or, "Where's the little Jewish actress?"

I was utterly horrified. I kept yelling back at him, "I'm a Christian, Swami!"

He stood over me, just like that huge Redwood tree of my dream, though not quite as comforting. He began to mimic me, like a distorted mirror in the fun house of an amusement park. He put his hands on his hips, widening his eyes and with his mouth forming a big circle he shouted "No? No? Junie is Irish, and Italian?"

I noticed that he called me Junie, not June. This was disturbing, as no one called me Junie, though it had been my childhood nickname! How did he know?

I cried for hours. I ran down to the Ganges river; the sound of the water rushing by always comforted me. But he sent someone to get me. Eyes downcast, I stood in front of him. Now he spoke quietly, gently, without the others present, "Who are you Junie? What is the truth of you?"

I said nothing. He continued, "In this life, you should accept, not reject who you are. That is the journey, you see?"

I started to cry again. "You are right," I admitted, finally. "My mother is Jewish."

He touched the top of my head lightly, with a little tap. "Don't wear a mask for others. We wear masks for others." Then he gave me an instruction that he reminded me of daily:

"Meditate, meditate, meditate!"

And he never brought any of this up again.

After dinner, in the early evening, he spoke to the group seated in a small circle. Before the satsang ended, he held up his forefinger, "One" he said, "we are all One. When a drop goes into the ocean, what happens? Infinity! Experience this."

He seemed to be looking directly at me, and I experienced a sudden rush of love for him. I remember feeling better about everything, curiously light-headed and peaceful. But this was only the beginning. Many layers of the onion needed to be peeled, along with a whole lot of tears!

Chapter 4

This wonderfully wild ride with Swami Rama would continue for 10 years, traveling all over India and Nepal, as well as studying at the Himalayan Institute in America. There were so many different kinds of lessons: some direct, some cryptic and some experiential. In Nepal, I learned to make do with much less sleep, and with his instruction, I would meditate from 3:30 to 6:00 a.m. and would then go to morning prayers. For the first time in my life, I had a glimpse of stillness, of peace. I learned about Homeopathy, vegetarian cooking for good health, and about the medical and scientific benefits of yoga. I was able to meet different families and visit local clinics. Swami Rama spoke to me of AIDS, the immune disorder that was killing so many people I knew. Years later, I would rely on all of this information when I found myself doing hospice work with the dying , as well as caring for and working with people with all kinds of illnesses, including AIDS.

But, along with the education, there came many more lessons in humility. Swami Rama always loved his gardens. When we were gardening, he would make me carry water buckets, or move rocks around, or tell me I could only "weed," as I wasn't sensitive enough yet to touch the flowers and make them grow. However, this practical work taught me everything I know about gardening! Today, I landscape my own land, planting trees, flowers, a water garden, fruits and vegetables. Swami Rama taught me respect for Nature: "Look, Junie! Look at that plant! See how many roots, buds, stems, leaves and blooms grow from this one plant."

Once I brought him a beautiful, hand-picked bouquet of flowers. I though he would be thrilled! But he did not appreciate it at all, and he turned away, saying, "You should never pick the flowers. Plants are also living things."

He had me do everyday chores like cooking, cleaning the kitchen and the bathrooms. He would burst in upon me suddenly, stand over me and say, "Are you saying your mantra, Junie?" Today, I love to cook for many people and clean my beautiful home. One day, he told me to go over to a very large tree and clean up all the leaves that had fallen—not all leaves, only those with no stems. Hours later, I went to him, saying, "I'm finished, Swamiji!" "Oh no! You're not," he said. He went over to the tree and shook it so that hundreds of leaves fell to the ground. "See, Junie? You are never finished. There will always be more leaves!"

Sometimes, he walked right past me, as if I wasn't there. At other times, he would publicly humiliate me. He was always animatedly arranging my marriage to some unfortunate man: "Oh look!" he would shout to anyone within earshot, "Junie's in love again!"

He seemed to know about my prior relationships. "Are you still in love with that airlines pilot? Don't be! Don't write to him! I know what he thinks, 'That Junie is crazy!'"

There was merciless teasing about Virat, one of his disciples, whom he thought I liked. Then the focus turned to Satish, one of our Indian guides. He would declare, "Junie will marry Satish this summer!" Or, "Junie is marrying Doctor B.!" He was referring to Dr.

Rudolph Ballentine Jr., the President of the Institute at that time.

He watched me fail at these relationships over the years. Then he stopped joking. "Are you a masochist?" he asked, pointedly. "Do you enjoy being beaten? You seek boyfriends because you are dreaming. This is Maya. Men do this with women, women do this with men. Give up men, Junie, you will use your energy much more wisely." If I still didn't get the lesson, he would excoriate me in front of the other students. When he saw me flirting one night, he seemed angry, "You seek the attention of men, you want them to look at you. You are vulgar!"

After that, I stayed away for days. He finally came over to me, "Why are you upset?" he asked, kindly. I looked at him, my eyes swollen from crying, "Why don't you like me?" He gave me a blank look asking, "Junie, do you have a father?" A loaded question, I knew. "Yes," I said, "You." "What?" he thundered. "You!" I said, a little louder. He smiled, sarcastically, "Oh, thank you, thank you! If I am your father, then why do you not listen to me?" "You called me vulgar!" I said. "You are always displeased with me!" He smiled, sweetly, "I am never displeased with you!"

At times he would appear furiously angry, but the very next moment he would be laughing. He could change shape, form and moods like a chameleon. I began to look at myself honestly, especially in relation to others. For example, I had a nasty habit of showing off. Because I had had music training, I tended to sing louder than the others during our chanting sessions. He finally made me stand up in front of the group and sing "Kumbaya my Lord" over and over again. He would make me perform constantly for anyone who would listen. He would make me tell the same joke repeatedly. No matter how many times everyone heard that joke, they would dutifully laugh loudly at the end, as if on cue! I finally got the point. I realized that I could drop this needy, attention-getting behavior. It was unnecessary to perform. I could just be myself, not the actress, nor the illusionist hiding behind an imposed personality. I began to question, "Who am I, really?" With all my defenses, walls, and emotional insecurities, how was I to know?

I became aware that he gave all of his students Indian names, like Kamal, Virat, Gopala, Samskriti, Sandhya, Arpita and Vimal. One night, I went over to him and asked him to give me an Indian name. Without hesitation, he said: "Pagli." All the Indians sitting there roared with laughter. He looked perfectly serious. Why did he always seem to be making fun of me? Later on, I went to one of the Indian ladies, and asked, "What does 'Pagli' mean?" "It means, 'crazy woman,'" she said, laughing.

Needless to say, I refused to use that name, or acknowledge anyone who tried to call me Pagli. He continued to call me Junie. Some months later, he said to me with very little expression in his voice, "You know, they called Mirabai, the singer-saint, Pagli? She was crazy with devotion to the Lord. This is a good name!"

But even after that he never called me Pagli, as if he were waiting for me to finally become "crazy with devotion."

Chapter 5

Swami Rama was not always so theatrical or dramatic in his dealings with me. Many times his instructions were gentle, quiet and direct. This was often the case during those rare moments when I sat at his feet without other people present. Once, I said to him, "Swamiji, I don't need a husband. I'll adopt a child on my own!!" He shook his head sadly, "Junie, Junie. Better you should only adopt me."

Another time he said to me, "You are a good girl and a fine artist — with a highly disorganized mind!" He told me to practice discipline of mind, action and speech, never to "speak anything without purpose, uselessly and untruthfully." At certain times, he was deliberately cryptic, obtuse, so I would have to search for the meaning of his words. He rarely initiated any physical contact with me, but on one occasion, he touched my throat, "This is important, Junie. Always come back here, to Vishuddha and visualize a clean, spiritual moon." Those words initially confused me, but later on, I understood the clarity, inspiration and limitless energy this point of focus brought to my life and work!

One sunny afternoon, I was working in his garden with another student. He came over to us and announced to her, "Junie will live alone, in a cave, all made of stone! You won't be able to go to Junie's house!" Ironically, years later, I purchased some acreage and lived in a cabin in the back woods, all made of stone! I spent a lot of time there, quietly alone. And in the winter, no one, including me, could get to my home—except on snow shoes.

One day I begged him to let me stay with him forever. I would give him everything I owned! Very directly, he said, "I don't want you to do this. I don't want what you own! You are a creative artist. So be creative, be free." Then, almost as an afterthought, "And, don't live in an ashram or community! This is not for you. Just visit!" Again, it took me several years to understand this instruction, because after Swamiji's passing, instead of heeding his warning, I joined another yoga community and dealt with all sorts of entanglements and problems there.

The last dream I had of Swami Rama was in California at yet another "crossroads" in my life. In my dream, I went to see him and knocked on the door. He opened it and looked very strange, not like himself—very thin, his eyes sunken deep in his face. He was wearing an unusual looking hat with a little brim. He told me I couldn't come in; he was leaving and not to be upset. He would still be there, but in a different way, I just wouldn't be able to see him. This dream was very real and powerful and when I woke up, I started to cry. My emotions were right at the surface of my conscious mind. I immediately called one of my friends at the Institute in Pennsylvania, who confirmed that he had passed away. I didn't think any more about this dream until years later, when someone showed me a picture of him before his mahasamadhi. There he was, sitting up and wearing this same funny hat, exactly as he had appeared in my dream!

This brought to mind the initial dream I had of Swami Rama years earlier when I knew that he would be my eternal friend. Everything comes full circle.

Chapter 6

Let me further explain the ways in which Swami Rama's teachings of yoga philosophy and psychology have furthered and influenced my life. It is sometimes difficult to put into words, because my time with him was so experiential and emotional. He taught me the very essence of yoga, and how connected it is to the body, mind and spirit.

First, he taught me how to breathe! Why, people ask, is this so important? He showed me how the breath is connected to the mind; how a pause in the breath, stopping the breath, comes from fear and that most fears originate in the mind. Bad, shallow, unsupported breathing creates stress in the body, and dis-ease. Through poor breathing habits, the body can become inactive and slothful. Bad breathing is oftentimes the beginning of disease.

He taught me how to sleep! At 3:30 a.m., in Rishikesh, he would say, "Wake Junie up! Sleep when you want to," he ordered, "not how long you think you should, but only as long as you need. Sleep should be under your control!" This practice has enabled me to get much more accomplished in my life. I used to have severe backaches and horrible nightmares. All that disappeared when I learned to sleep fewer hours.

The influence Swamiji has had on us and the way he has touched so many lives, is really amazing and crosses all barriers, races, and people. Swamiji once said to me, " Junie, do not make a god out of me. I am a human being, I am also a person." I think he said this because I was beginning to idolize him. People falling at his feet and worshipping him like a deity could be misconstrued as cultism. Swamiji did not want this. I always recognized the Divine in him. I also think that those who worshipped him had their own idealized image of him, which led to disappointments, not so much in his actions, but their own expectations. I saw signs of this always. He was very much against such expectations.

He would instruct me about nonattachment. I would be upset if he, or the others, ignored me. I was always concerned about what people would say about me, if they loved me or hated me, or even if they didn't smile at me! He showed me how to be independent of the opinions of others and how to undertake the inner journey through a healthy understanding of myself. He taught me not to rely on others for my happiness. He explained that there is no such thing as loneliness. We are born alone and die alone. Lonely feelings can be transformed into contemplation, peace and solitude. This way of life can lead to inner personal contentment.

Through Swamiji's teachings, I became less immersed in the need for the gross objects of the world, and the seductive aspects of success and fame. He often spoke of death and life, of how to grieve when someone or something we love dies. He taught that both death and life are to be accepted equally, like equal acceptance of good and bad. It became important for me to learn how to "take the middle path" in life, rather than to walk so precipitously close to the edge.

He loved Nature and taught me how to be in tune with the natural world, to learn from and appreciate the value of the earth and everything that lives and grows on it.

He laughed when I wouldn't speak because I was "practicing silence." "Never do these things for show, Junie, to impress others." I learnt how to be a bit more understated and helpful, with no expectation of kudos or rewards.

As to my career as an actress, the most valuable gift that he gave me was how to use the "masks" of my personality in my work—but to learn to differentiate these masks from the masks I used to hide behind, in my personal life. He showed me how these other masks would keep me in ignorance of the truth and hinder my own spiritual growth.

"Slow down," he would say. "We need to learn to be more still." With some of the tasks he made me perform, he showed me how to use the difficult experiences of life as teachings; how certain failures could lead to further self-knowledge and transformation. He asked, "Do you know whether the violence and the destruction of the world also lie within you? Do you take responsibility for your perceptions or do you hunt only for pleasure?"

Through self-knowledge one can truly become free and know the truth. One night, we had a bonfire and satsang. I went to him in a quiet moment. I said, "I am not beautiful, Swamiji." He stared at me, "Everyone is beautiful," he said. "You are beautiful. You are YOU!" He then gave me a pile of sticks and told me to offer them into the fire, "Offer everything to the fire of knowledge at the Guru Chakra." I know now what he meant by this.

Greatest of all, he taught me how to meditate! This is the ultimate gift that he gave me, the answer to most of life's questions and difficulties. Mindfulness through mantra has helped me to perceive the universe differently, taught me how to listen in silence to the innermost part of me. This is how I recognize that I also have an inner teacher who will keep me in the present moment, the now, and allow me to let go of the past, and will keep my mind one-pointed. If I can continue on this path, no matter how imperfectly, then Swami Rama has not wasted a moment of his time with me.

Chapter 7

Why do I write all this now?

Perhaps it is because this great man understood and perceived life on life's terms, unlike anyone I had ever known. Perhaps it is my desire to keep his teachings alive in the present moment, to re-evaluate all that I learned from him, with the realization that so much of what he said came true—full circle—in my life today.

What did I learn? Volumes!

Joy, music, focus of energy, direction, silence, discipline, clean living, self-respect, gardening, service, truthfulness, nonattachment, freedom, creativity and acceptance! I have goals in my life today: to care for others, to be compassionate, to teach what I have learned, and at the same time to cultivate myself as an artist.

Am I perfect? Have I arrived at the top of the mountain, at the pinnacle of enlightenment? God, no! I am ever trudging. If there is one thing I understand from my teacher, it is that, "there are always more leaves" under that tree of life to clean up; there is always more work to do! I am the perennial traveler and student. I make mistakes and stumble; but even if I fall, his words are always there to keep me from drowning, so I can reach the other side of the river. But there are many rivers to cross. He gave me a way to accept my past and grow and learn from it;

to understand my life's journey, no matter how unconventional. And the greatest thing he did for me was to not "fetter me to the boat." He let me go! He gave me his blessing and sent me on my way to continue the journey, on my own, but with confidence. I am sure that I will never achieve the devotion of Pagli Mirabai or the renunciation and wisdom of Mother Teresa; but at least trudging the path of right action has brought me peace, inner strength and love.

There is a beautiful passage that comes to mind, from Vishwa Sara Tantra, called "Hymn to the Guru." The author speaks about the "perfect Guru, free from earthly bondage, beyond life's sweet and bitter, eternal, witness of the mind's moods and motions." He ends with these words, "How shall thought compass, or tongue describe Him?"

I have heard many words describe Swami Rama: words of love, devotion, joy, anger, bitterness, blame, jealousy, laughter and exasperation. I cannot judge anyone else's experience. I only have my own. And I know that wherever I am and whatever life has in store for me, his words will always be there to guide me—as long as I remember, as St. Benedict said, "to listen and attend with the ear of my heart."

Shri Roshan Lal Kanodia

*

Swami Rama: My Mother, Father, Guru and God

Shri Roshan Lal Kanodia

Shri Roshal Lal, a successful businessman of Kanpur associated with sugar and vegetable merchandising, was born in Kanpur in the year 1937. He passed out of high school in 1949 and it was during his high school years that he first met Swami Rama at Anasuya Ghat, Chitrakoot. At that time, Swami Rama was known as Patti Wale Baba or Leaf Baba because he survived on leaves from the hanging branches of trees. Roshan Lalji visited Patti Wale Baba every Sunday for about five to six months before the Baba disappeared and his whereabouts were unknown. Roshan Lal made his re-acquaintance with Swami Rama, known then as Bhole Baba, at Jajmau, Kanpur in 1960. He visited Bhole Baba for about four years, but every time Bhole Baba would send him away, saying, "I have no time now," or, "Come tomorrow," or "Come back later." Only after 1964, did Roshan Lal become closely associated with Swami Rama.

Roshan Lalji served the Himalayan Institute of Yoga Science and Philosophy, Kanpur as its Treasurer from 1968 to 1996 and as Vice President from 1996 to the present. He was also the Treasurer of the Himalayan Institute Hospital Trust, Jolly Grant from 1989 to 1994 and Treasurer of Sadhana Mandir Trust, Rishikesh from 1970 to 1996. Roshan Lalji is a member of the Kanpur Sugar Merchant Association and served as the Secretary of the Social Welfare Association of Kanpur from 1950 to 1958.

My Early Experiences with Swami Rama

Invocation:

Akhanda-mandalakaram vyaptam yena characharam
Tatpadam darshitam yena. Tasmai shri guruavenamah.

My salutations to that Guru who revealed to me That (Brahman) which is indivisible and which pervades the entire universe, moving and unmoving.

My first darshan of Pujya (worthy of worship) Swamiji (Swami Rama) was in the year 1948. At that time, the father of one of my friends was transferred to Karvi and I used to go there every Saturday to meet my friend. On Sundays, my friend and I would go to Anusuya Ghat in Chitrakoot. There I had my first darshan of Pujya Swamiji. At that time, he was known as Patti Wale Baba because he survived on leaves from the hanging branches of trees. He also used to keep both arms upraised as a form of austerity. I visited him every Sunday for about five to six months. All of a sudden, he disappeared without a trace. I, therefore, stopped visiting Chitrakoot. We came to know much later that he had become a Shankaracharya. After being a Shankaracharya for only two to three years, he left that ceremonial position and returned.

In the year 1960, there was a naga sadhu who used to stand in front of the Jajmau Siddhnath Temple. One of my friends, Dr. Pratap Narayan Rastogi, was very fond of visiting saints and sages. I went with him to have darshan of the naga sadhu. There was a huge crowd around him. I told my friend, "We have had darshan, but it is difficult to ask questions of the sadhu because of the crowd." The sadhu asked us to come back the next day to ask our questions. We returned the next day at 4:00 a.m. We sat there from 4:00 a.m. to 8:00 a.m. At 8:00 a.m., when people started arriving, Dr. Pratap and I went away to the Siddhnath Shiva temple for darshan. There, many people who knew me asked me how and why I had come. I told them that I had come to have darshan of the Naga Baba. They informed me that a renowned saint called Bhole Baba was staying in the gardens of Mata Deen Bhagwan Das and that I could have his darshan.

When we went there, we learnt that he had gone away to the city. I told Dr. Pratap that we should come back that night. That night, at 10:30 p.m., Dr. Pratap and I went back to see the saint. We realized that Bhole Baba was none other than Swami Rama, formerly known as Patti Wale Baba. He was dictating to one Dr. S. N. Agnihotri on the spiritual heart. After about 10 minutes, he looked towards us and said, "You have come." We said, "Yes Master, we have come." Then he got up and came over to us. He asked us which city we had come from and then asked with annoyance, "Is this the right time to come? If something bad were to happen to you en route, I'll get a bad name. Come back tomorrow at 1:00 p.m."

Dr. Pratap used to close his dispensary daily at 1:30 p.m. The next day he closed up at 1:00 p.m., and by 1:30 p.m we reached the garden where Swamiji was staying. Swamiji used to have his lunch at that time, after which he would rest up to 4:00 p.m. We waited around and came back to be with Swamiji at 4:00 p.m. This routine continued for six days. On the seventh day, Dr. Pratap wanted to have tea at Meera

Restaurant before going to visit Swamiji. While having tea at Meera Restaurant, Dr. Pratap decided to have a dosa as well. I refused to eat before having darshan. Dr. Pratap had his dosa and tea and we then reached Swamiji. On that day too, Swamiji w about to have his lunch when we arrived. Starting eat, he asked us, "Will you have some food?" I replied, "We have already had our food." Dr. Pratap advised me to take a small offering of food as prasad. But after having prasad, I grew very hungry. After a while, Swamiji again asked me to have food. I again lied, saying that we had already eaten. After his asking the second time, I felt even hungrier. Swamiji again asked me a third time to have food with him and I lied again. By now, my hunger was reaching its peak. Swamiji remarked, "Don't you feel ashamed, lying to me? You are miserable because of your hunger and yet you keep telling me that you have had your food." He then asked the cook to bring some food for me. Food was served and I ate with Swamiji. After lunch, he wanted to rest and asked me to massage his feet which I did until 4:00 p.m.

At 4:00 p.m., he woke up and asked me, "Son, whose feet do you massage at home?" I told him that I used to massage my father's feet. He then began to question me about my life and also provided the answers before I could respond. When I was six months old, I lost my mother and was looked after by my grandmother. My grandmother died in 1946. Whenever a group of children used to fight amongst themselves, their parents used to come to defend them. I had no parents to defend me, and this used to upset me. Swamiji understood this and that I felt alone. He said, "From now onwards, I am both your father and mother." He continued to ask me many questions about my life and continued to provide the answers as well. After that he asked me to leave. He told me that I could meet him whenever I wanted to. However, after that, I could not have his darshan for another three or four years.

While visiting Swamiji with Dr. Pratap at the gardens of Mata Deen Bhagwan Das, I learnt from Dr. Pratap that Tula Ram Gupta, whose shop was close to our grocery shop, met with an accident on his motorcycle and had to have his foot amputated. Suddenly, a fear filled my heart that I too would meet the same fate and would have my foot amputated. In the grip of this fear, I reached Swamiji's place. As soon he saw me, he started saying, "Hey, accidents keep happening, but I am telling you that your foot will not be amputated." I wondered how Swamiji knew of my fearful thoughts.

A year later, while visiting the Siddhnath Temple on the day of Durga Mangal, I was involved in a motorcycle accident around 1:00 a.m. and injured my foot. In spite of this injury, I continued to the temple for darshan. On reaching home, I checked my injured foot, cleaned the wound, applied some oil to it and went to sleep. But when I woke up around 7:00 a.m. the next morning, I found that I could not move my feet. There was no sensation in both feet. I covered myself with a sheet and started crying thinking that while I had feared amputation of one foot, now, both feet had become useless.

A Babu Pahalwan (wrestler/body builder) used to live in Mool Gunj. He was an arrogant man. He suddenly showed up, God only knows how, asking, "Brother, it is 8:00 a.m., why are you still lying in bed?" I told him about my accident and the problem with my feet. He was a master at treating bone injuries. He examined me and applied some medicine. This continued for about seven to ten days. I don't know how, but today, I am walking on my feet and have no problems with my feet.

My Experiences with Swamiji in Kanpur

I again had the opportunity to visit Swamiji when he began to visit the home of Dr. Sunandabai in Kanpur. Seeing me coming from a distance, he would say, "I have no time, come back tomorrow." I began to think that Swamiji no longer wanted to see me. Once, when Swamiji had come to Kanpur, I told my friend, Bal Mukund Ambani, that a great saint had arrived in Kanpur and that he could have his darshan using my name as a reference. So he went there, using me as a reference. Swamiji spoke to him for almost an hour and a half. Swamiji kept asking my friend about me, wondering when I was likely to visit him. Upon returning, my friend told me that Swamiji kept asking about me the whole time.

I found out that the time for Swamiji's darshan was between 10:00 a.m. and 11:00 a.m. It was the month of Shravan and I used to go daily to the Siddhi Vinayak temple, returning only at around 2:00 p.m. So I decided to have Swamiji's darshan after the month of Shravan. When Shravan was over, I enquired about Swamiji's availability. I left home at 9:30 a.m., bought 30-40 kg. of fruit, perched the fruit on the petrol tank of my motorcycle and drove towards Dr. Sunandabai's bungalow to visit Swamiji. En route, it started raining heavily. I felt extremely cold and started to shiver. I began to wonder if I should turn back. However, with determination, I decided that no matter what, I would not return without seeing Swamiji; even if I had to go hungry all day. But I had another concern. How would I prevent the heavy bag of fruits from falling off when I reached and tried to get off the bike? Worrying thus, I reached Dr. Sunandabai's bungalow. As soon as I reached, Swamiji came out, picked up the bag and took it inside.

There were three other persons inside with him, S. R. Kharbanda, Inspector of Income Tax, Mr. Manohar Lal Juneja and one other gentleman. Swamiji introduced me to all of them as his son, showing them the nice fruits I had brought. He distributed one fruit to each of them and then asked them to leave. Pointing to me, he said that he needed to speak to me. Everybody left, except Mr. Manohar Lal Juneja. Swamiji asked him to leave too, stating that he had something important to discuss with me. Mr. Manohar Lal Juneja was reluctant to leave. Swamiji finally told him, "If you want to stay, then I will leave." At this, Mr. Juneja left. Swamiji then called the watchman, asked him to lock the door and tell anyone who came by that Swamiji had left for Lucknow. Then Swamiji went into the kitchen, prepared halwa and roasted some papad and made me eat all of it, while having me sit, like a child, on his lap. After this, from the fruits I had taken for him, he took out two mangoes, cut them open with a knife and showed me how to eat the mango using a spoon. While eating, he told me many times to visit him whenever I wanted to, without any hesitation. Thus, I again had darshan of Pujya Swamiji. When I asked him about his disappearance from Chitrakoot, he replied, "Son, I became a Shankaracharya, after which I was a Professor at Prayag University. I kept moving from one place to another." I then asked him why he used to keep his arms upraised at that time. He told me that he was Dandi Swami Ram and had to undertake an act of penance for having renounced his status as a Dandi Swami.

Once at 1:30 a.m., I was sitting by Swamiji's side in Dr. Sunandabai's bungalow. In the room where Swamiji used to stay, there was a door opening through a balcony to the road outside. The room also had an entry door from the inside of the house. At night, I sensed someone peeping in from the outside door. After that, I sensed somebody peeping in from the other door. I did not want to give Swamiji any inkling of my feelings. Swamiji asked me, "Son, is somebody peeping in?" I said, "Yes." He said, "Go and check to see who is there." I went from there towards the road; there was no one. Then he asked, "Was somebody peeping at the other door too?" I said, "Yes." I then went towards that door also, and upon checking told him that there was no one there either. After almost half an hour, Swamiji asked me to go and make him some tea. To get to the kitchen, I had to go through the balcony, a passage way, downstairs, and then through another balcony, switching lights on and off as I proceeded. After making tea, I came back upstairs with the tea for Swamiji. Swamiji asked me, "Son, did you meet anybody on the way? I hope your fear has not spoiled the tea." Then after taking a sip, he said, "No, the tea is alright." Then after a while, he asked me, "Do you know who was peeping?" I said, "No." Then he told me that it was the fear in me that was peeping out!

Dr. Sunandabai used to leave in the morning after breakfast and used to return around 1:30 p.m. Upon returning from the medical college or hospital, she liked to have her lunch right away. She used to ask Swamiji to have lunch the moment she got back and never used to allow any outsider to be by Swamiji's side while he ate his lunch. The exceptions to this

rule were Dr. Uma Mehrotra, Ram Tandon and me.
That day, when Dr. Sunandabai asked Swamiji if she
should bring his lunch, Swamiji agreed and asked her
to bring it. When she had gone to bring the food for
Swamiji, somebody knocked on the door. Swamiji
asked me to open the door. I tried to refuse, telling
him that Dr. Sunandabai was about to bring him his
lunch. Swamiji scolded me and asked me to open the
door, which I did. There were about 15-20 students
from the Indian Institute of Technology (I.I.T.) at
Kanpur who had come to meet Swamiji. They were
there for almost one and a half hours. Hearing
their voices, Dr. Sunandabai also came up and sat
with them. They started having some irrelevant
discussions with Swamiji who kept listening to them
patiently, even agreeing with their opinions. Even
though (in Swamiji's opinion), I do not know English,
I realized that the students were trying to make a fool
of Swamiji. And even though Dr. Sunandabai did not
know Hindi very well, she too felt bad that these boys
were trying to fool Swamiji. She knew Swamiji well,
and understood that he was aware of what was going
on. In spite of this, Swamiji continued to humor them
and agree with their opinions. When they left after
one and a half hours, Dr. Sunandabai thought that
Swamiji would skip his lunch, as it was late. However,
the moment those boys left, Swamiji started yelling,
"Oh! Because of Sunandabai, I am dying of hunger."
Dr. Sunandabai said, "Somebody comes to meet you
and he opens the door (pointing towards me). How
dare he open the door without your permission?"
Swamiji said, "Go and bring my food Sunanda. Today
you should bring your food also and eat with me."
When they started eating, Dr. Sunandabai declared,
"Swamiji, this is all your drama." Swamiji started
laughing loudly and said, "Sunanda, sometimes we

enjoy making a fool of others." This led us to realize that Swamiji, knowing well what was happening, had pretended he did not know. He had fooled the boys, rather than the other way around. Interestingly, after about eight to ten days, all those boys came back and asked for forgiveness from Swamiji. After that, Swamiji gave many lectures at I.I.T. This shows how Swamiji often pretended not to know, while knowing everything fully well.

I had gone to receive Swamiji at Delhi along with 10 to 12 other people from Kanpur including Shri Gauri Nath Tandon and Dr. Khanna. I thought that Swamiji liked me very much. In the same way, the others too, felt in their hearts that Swamiji liked them best. However, without directly revealing their inner feelings, they started commenting that Swamiji liked so and so more than he liked them. We received Swamiji, and proceeded with him to the Lodhi Hotel. In the evening, Swamiji was sitting with us as we sat around him on the carpet. All of a sudden, Swamiji said, "Why do you feel that Swamiji likes you very much? You think Swamiji likes him (pointing to one of us), and he thinks Swamiji likes you. I do not belong to the one who gave me birth; so how can I be yours? I love you all."

Swamiji told me that in the year 1966, I would have my own business. I just laughed. He asked me why I was laughing. I said, "Sir, I am in the sugar business. I can only raise ten to twenty thousand rupees. There is no way I can manage to raise three to four hundred thousand rupees to start my own business." Swamiji asked, "Don't you believe me?" I replied, "No, no, it's not that." He asked me to just wait and see. In the year 1958, a work colleague and I decided to establish a firm with the name, "Roshan Lal & Company." It would be a partnership and we would share the

profits equally. It was also decided that I would bear
the initial monthly expenses. For the first three years,
I used to pay myself a salary of only Rs. 50 per month.
Over the next three years, I took Rs. 300 per month.
By 1966, the firm had amassed a large sum of money.
I decided to buy out my partner and was expecting
to retain an amount of Rs. 200,000 to 300,000. The
accounts of our firm had not been audited and cleared
from 1958 to 1966. Whatever profits we had earned
had been shared with my partner. In February 1966, I
needed some money. When I asked my partner for the
money, he put me off for months without complying.
When I asked him to clear my dues, he said, "What
dues?" At that time, there were sugar stocks in my
shop worth around Rs. 500,000 which belonged to the
partnership. I could have held on to those stocks but
I did not want people to think that I was a cheat. So I
sold the stocks and shared the money with my partner.
I was again refused my dues. This went on for two to
three months. It was already August of 1966 and I was
reminded of Swamiji's prediction that I would have
my own business that same year. Instead, whatever
business was going on had also come to a standstill.
There was no source of income. I was reduced to a
hand-to-mouth existence.

Several days later, I went to meet the District
Supply Officer who asked me why I had not picked
up my sugar stocks for the last two to three months.
I was quiet. He knew that the partnership was not
doing well and offered to help me. He encouraged me
to start my own business. I went to visit one of my
relatives in Arya Nagar. His wife also asked, "Brother,
why are you not picking up your sugar stocks for
the last two to three months?" I told her that in the
rainy season, stocks were damp. I would collect my
stocks later, when they were dry. Then she said, "We

have heard that because of lack of funds you are not collecting the stocks." I denied all this. She gave me Rs.10,000, saying that it was better to utilize the money than have it lying in the bank. When I reached home, I found Shri U. N. S., Accountant from the DSO Office, who looked upon me like a brother, waiting for me. He took out Rs. 20,000 from his pocket and said, "I have sold off the land in my village. You keep this money and utilize it in your business." I now had Rs. 30,000 with me. I calculated that with this money, I could buy 260 sacks of sugar at the controlled rate. I went to the DM's office and said, "Sir, with your blessings I have been able to arrange money for 260 sacks. He gave me a permit for 260 sacks at the controlled rate and I immediately collected the stocks. After collecting the sacks of sugar, the DM asked me to sell off the sugar on the open market at the much higher market rate. I was speechless and kept standing there. He called the Inspector who tried to explain how this worked. I was worried about doing this. Finally, Shri U. N. S. also gave me the same advice. I sold those stocks off. I had bought the stocks for Rs. 30,000 and by selling them, I now had Rs. 160,000. With this money, I bought 1000 sacks of sugar, which I again sold at market rates. By such transactions, my business started flourishing. After six or seven months, an officer called me and asked me how my business was running. I told him that the business was running smoothly. Now, the market rate had dropped to Rs. 325. He advised me to buy back from the market the initial 260 sacks of sugar that I had got from the DSO at the controlled rate and sold on the open market. He gave me a permit for this transaction. I was thus able to clear my conscience and be free of any worries on this account. By now, I had amassed a capital of Rs. 250,000 and the business was established on a firm basis, just as Swamiji had predicted. It is evident that all this was possible only with the intervention and support of divine powers.

I knew that every year Swamiji used to go to Mansarovar in Tibet. But I never knew when he would go there. In 1972 or 1973, I told him, "You go to Maansarovar every year. Why can't you take me along?" He replied that he would take me along this time. About 10 to 15 of us went to the Delhi airport to see Swamiji off. He had a ticket on an American airline and we accompanied him to the gate after he had checked in his luggage and collected his boarding pass. Except me, everybody else thought that Swamiji was going to America. I was just not that educated and knew only what I was told. From the airport, we went to the Lodhi Hotel. The Manager of the hotel, Mr. R. D. Gupta, requested me to escort his wife from Delhi to Kanpur. I had to visit Rishikesh first, after which we left for Kanpur. When I reached Kanpur, Mrs. Gupta wanted to meet Dr. Khanna. After breakfast, I took Mrs. Gupta to Dr. Khanna's home on Vihana Road. The moment I reached there, Dr. Khanna told me, "Oh dear! If you had come a minute earlier, you could have spoken to Swamiji who called from Japan." I felt quite offended that Swamiji had lied to me. Though Dr. Khanna invited me to stay for tea, I made some excuse and came away, quite angry at Swamiji. The moment I reached home, my wife called out to me from the terrace saying that there was a call from Swamiji. He had given a number in Kathmandu and asked me to call him back on that number. I booked the call. The moment I booked the call, Mr. L. K. Mishra from America came to see me and said that Swamiji had told him that his whereabouts would be known only to me. Nobody else would know where Swamiji was. I told him that I had booked a call to Kathmandu but was not able to contact Swamiji. I then requested a person I knew in the telephone department to help me get the call through. He advised me to go to Delhi as it would be difficult to contact Nepal from Kanpur. Mr. L. K. Mishra and I left for Delhi and booked the call from there. Then it suddenly occurred to me that it would be far easier and cheaper to go directly to Kathmandu ourselves! The next day we left for Kathmandu. On reaching Kathmandu, we called the number that Swamiji had given us. We were told that they knew who Swamiji was, but that Swamiji had not come there. We went there anyway and after many phone calls, we got Swamiji's address and immediately took a taxi to that address. There, an old man got annoyed when we enquired about Swamiji and asked us to leave. I suddenly remembered that my wife's cousin was a secretary in the law department in Kathmandu. We went there and explained the language problems we were facing and our difficulties in tracing Swamiji. Poor chap, he too tried to phone many places but was not successful in finding Swamiji's whereabouts. When we came out of his bungalow, we saw a parked car with Swamiji sitting in it! I started shouting in my excitement. Swamiji asked me not to make a nuisance of myself with all this shouting. He asked us to sit in the car and took us to the same bungalow whose old caretaker had chased us away. I told him that we had come there earlier. He said it was alright as nobody there knew him. He took me upstairs and served me some rather spicy food. I then started massaging his feet. While I was doing so, he asked me whether I had had darshan of the Pashupatinath temple. He asked me to be ready by six o'clock the next morning. It began to rain very heavily and I was feeling very cold. Having come to Nepal without preparation, I did not have any woollens. In the morning, when I washed my hands, they became numb. When I brushed my teeth, my mouth also became numb. When I took my bath, my whole body became numb. Somehow, I put on my clothes and opened the door. As soon as I opened the door, I found Swamiji standing there asking me if I had taken my bath. I told him that I had and he wrapped me in his shawl. That shawl was very warm, as if there was a heater inside it; it helped my numb body to thaw out comfortably. I got ready and came downstairs with Swamiji. There was a car parked outside which took us to the Pashupatinath Temple. The Mahantji of the temple came to greet Swamiji and let us in through a special gate near the river. Swamiji asked the Mahantji to allow me to have the prasad from the temple. After this, Swamiji asked the Mahantji to show me the rosary of one-faced Rudrakash beads, the south-faced conch, the holy nagmani and many other holy relics like the paras stone which was buried in the ground there. On coming out after darshan, Swamiji distributed a lot of money to the beggars. Then Swamiji took me to the nearby Gujreshwari Devi Temple, telling me that the pilgrimage is incomplete if one does not visit this temple after Pashupatinath darshan. When we got back, Swamiji told me that he would have liked to take me to Mansarovar, but that the weather was getting inclement and I would have breathing problems there. He promised to take me there some other time. He took out two air tickets from his bag for our return flight.

Some Incredible Experiences with Swamiji

When Swamiji used to take rest in his room, people were not allowed to go in without permission. There were only two or three persons (Uma Mehrotra, Ram Tandon and me), who were allowed to go in while Swamiji was resting. One day, I entered Swamiji's room without knocking and I was aghast at what I saw. Both arms and both legs were separated from his body. I was dumbstruck. Noticing me, he quickly re-attached his limbs and sat up. I noticed that his eyes were very red. He said, "Ah! So you have come, son." I said I was sorry for my intrusion. He did not say anything except, "No, no, it's O.k." I was astonished. Later, in 1968, he took me to the Kali Ghat Temple in Calcutta. In the front section of the temple, there lived a painter upstairs. Swamiji introduced him to me, saying, "Son, he is the guru who taught me how to detach limbs."

One day Swamiji asked me if I had seen the divine form of Ardhanarishwar, the conjoined form of Shiva and Shakti, half man and half woman. I started laughing, thinking he was joking. He said, "O.k. Come over tomorrow and I will show you." The next day, when I went to see him, he was smoking a cigarette while seated on a blanket on the floor. He kept on rubbing a sword with one hand and asked me, "Would you like to see the divine form of Ardhanarishwar?" He asked me this question three times and while asking me this the third time, the limbs on the left side of his body became absolutely white, while the limbs on the right side became absolutely dark. He explained that Parvati or Shakti was fair, while Shankar or Shiva was dark. The left side of the body was female, and right side male. This was the divine form of Ardhanarishwar. Then he asked Dr. Pratap, who was also there, "Are you watching?" Dr. Pratap replied in the affirmative. Then Swamiji instructed Dr. Pratap to take out a pen from his pocket and poke its nib into the left side of Swamiji's body. There was no bleeding. Swamiji said, "Look, I have transferred blood from the left side to the right side. That is why the right side has become dark and the left side has turned white. So when you poked the pen's nib into the left side, there was no bleeding because I have drained all of the blood out from that side."

Swamiji then asked me, "Son, have you seen the third eye of Lord Shiva?" On my denial, he asked me to go with him to the room upstairs. He sat down and instructed me to cover him with the seven or eight blankets that were lying there. I opened out each blanket and covered him completely. Then he told me not to come in front of him. If I wanted to ask any question, I should keep it in front of his face on the opposite wall. After some time, I noticed that his whole body was trembling; then from within there came a light. He asked, "Son, have you seen this?" Again there were tremors in his body and the light vanished. He said, "Quick, remove the blankets, I am suffocating." I removed all the blankets. He thus showed me the divine form of Ardhanarishwar and the third eye of Lord Shiva.

I was once diagnosed with stones in my gall bladder. I wanted to get operated and got myself admitted to a hospital. However, as an anesthesiologist was not available, the surgery had to be postponed. One day, I was asleep at home. Swamiji appeared in my dream accompanied by a doctor. Swamiji asked me, "How come you are lying down?" I told him that I had gallstones and needed to have an operation. Swamiji asked me, "Shall we do your operation?" I replied, "Yes, please do." I felt like I was taken and made to stand outside my own body. Swamiji opened a bag that he had with him, took out surgical instruments and started the operation. After the operation, Swamiji showed me the stones he had taken out saying, "See, this is it." Then he stitched me up. After stitching me up, Swamiji washed his hands and feet with hot water, like doctors do after an operation. Then he said,"O.k., give us some tea and we will leave." My wife brought tea which they drank and left. All this was part of my dream.

Very early the next morning, Dr. Pratap Narayan, a Homeopathic doctor known to Swamiji, came to ask about my health. I told him that the operation had been done. The doctor said, "Your operation has been done and you have been absolved of your sins. Now, you should follow Swamiji's instructions. For the next six months, no roaming around, and no lifting of heavy objects." For four or five days I did as instructed. After that I started working again. One day, it was raining and my car got stuck. Physically, I am quite strong and I gave the car a push from behind. While doing so, I hurt my hand and saw blood oozing out from the wound. The wound then got infected and I started having a fever. Swamiji came to Kanpur and stayed at Dr. Sunandabai's home but refused to meet me. My fever wouldn't come down. When the fever continued for three to four months, I became very weak. Then, one day Swamiji came. He had a bag with him, which I recognized as the bag from which he had taken out the surgical instruments in my dream. Swamiji gave me some medicine and I recovered. There was a music system in the bag. Swamiji left the bag with me and even today I have that bag. If you have faith, you will believe my experience.

Once, when we were returning from Tikamgarh, Swamiji told me, "Son, today I will give you darshan of Chausat Yogini (64 Yoginis) in Khajuraho." In Khajuraho, Swamiji made me stand at a particular place and asked me to rotate on my heel and look around me. I took the turn, without quite understanding. Then, Swamiji asked me if I had seen a Sri Yantra? I said, "Yes, I have seen a Sri Yantra." He said just as there is continuity without a break in the Sri Yantra, there is continuity in the hills around here also. The Sri Yantra is right here, somewhere. Swamiji then asked a man he knew to take me to the Chausat Yogini Temple. He said he would meet us there. The man informed us that the usual route to the temple was closed and we would have to take a longer route. With Swamiji's flight schedule, there was not enough time; Swamiji told me that he would take me there some other time. I wondered in my inner heart whether my turn for this darshan would ever come. Thinking thus, I left for Kanpur while Swamiji went to Delhi.

When I went to Delhi from Kanpur, Swamiji asked me why I had wondered whether I would ever have a darshan of the Chausat Yogini temple. He told me that I would have the darshan the very next day. He asked me to go to the residence of Mr. Anand Pratap Singh and to get the room at the back emptied and cleaned. He said, "I want to give you this darshan there itself. I also want Anand Pratap Singh and Pandit Rajmani to be there for the darshan." By chance, Dr. Usharbudh Arya (now Swami Ved Bharati), happened to also come there. So all four of us were asked by Swamiji to reach Mr. Anand Pratap's residence by 6:00 a.m. Swamiji told me, "Son I want you to keep whatever appears there." I asked Swamiji to explain, but he did not reply. I went to Anand Pratap's residence, got the room emptied and cleaned. The next day, all four of us reached the place early and waited for Swamiji. Swamiji came on time and instructed the four of us to stand in the four corners of the room. He asked us to meditate on Divine Mother and said he was leaving to take a bath in the bathroom next door. Swamiji hung up his bag on the door and without taking off the kurta and dhoti he was wearing, he went and stood under the shower. While standing there, he shouted out to us to keep meditating on the Divine Mother. The moment he shouted, there was a loud sound like a bomb blast. That sudden blast made us open our eyes and we saw flowers scattered all over the floor; in the center, there was a Sri Yantra. Swamiji came running out, continuously chanting, and showed us the Sri Yantra. He distributed a few flowers amongst us and told us we could use these flowers for special rituals in our own homes, but not to give them to others. He then said, "Anand is pre-occupied with politics throughout the day. He will not be able to worship this Sri Yantra. Usharbudh keeps travelling; he too will not be able to worship it. Rajmani also keeps on moving around, so he too will not be able to do the worship. This fellow (me), stays at home, he will be able to worship the Sri Yantra. What is the opinion of the three of you?" They said it was alright by them. Swamiji took out a red handkerchief from his bag, tied the Sri Yantra in it, and told me to safeguard it. Thus I had darshan of Sri Yantra. This Sri Yantra was with me from then until 1993. In the year 1993, Swamiji took the Sri Yantra from me and gave it to Anand Swami. That Sri Yantra is now being worshipped at Narayangarh where Anand Swami has established the Swami Rama Trust.

Experiences with Swamiji
at HIHT

There used to be a lot of snakes around the Himalayan Institute Hospital Trust (HIHT) campus. They were very big snakes, about 20 feet long, but they never harmed anyone. At that time, the construction of the guest house was going on. The laborers happened to kill a snake during the construction. Swamiji was not told about it by anyone; he got to know about it somehow. He became extremely angry and to show his anger, he stopped phoning us. After a week, there was a phone call from Swamiji. Swamiji scolded me severely for the mishap and instructed me to perform a ritual to atone for the death of the snake. The ritual involved a lot of milk and I did as instructed. Only after the ritual was performed did Swamiji's anger subside.

It was winter time; maybe it was October or November. There was active construction going on at HIHT. At that time, there wasn't any good way of communicating with Swamiji when he was away in America. In those days, Swamiji would spend most of his time in Pennsylvania. At an appointed time, between 6:30 p.m. and 7:00 p.m. we would go to Mr. Garg's house in Dehradun to receive Swamiji's call from Pennslyvania. Mrs. Soni, the wife of Lt. General Soni, used to live next to the HIHT campus. We were engaged in some land-related litigation with Mrs. Soni. Around 6:00 p.m., Mrs. Soni was on her way to her lawyer's house. Just before she reached Doiwala, her car skidded badly, causing an accident. Mrs. Soni was taken to the hospital. I went over to Mr. Garg's house to inform him about this accident and we were discussing whether we should visit her in the hospital even though we were involved in a legal dispute with her. At that moment, the phone rang. It was Swamiji calling from Pennsylvania. We told him about Mrs. Soni's accident. Swamiji responded right away, "She is dead; she is no more." The accident must have taken place a little after 6:00 p.m. and Swamiji's call came around 6:45 p.m. With the state of phone communications in those days, there was no way that Swamiji could have learnt about the accident and Mrs. Soni's death. However, Swamiji was already aware of the accident and Mrs. Soni's death, despite being thousands of miles away in America.

I considered the leftover food in Swamiji's plate as prasad and would not eat my breakfast till I could have these leftovers. I was pacing to and fro, waiting for Swamiji to finish his breakfast. Mr. Garg and a friend were visiting Swamiji and were sitting with him. Swamiji must have sensed my agitation and asked, "Son, what's the matter?" I replied, "Swamiji, we have to make a lot of payments and there is no money." Swamiji got very angry. "You people insult me. Am I sitting here to be insulted?" As Swamiji was extremely angry, I decided to go away. Later, I heard from Mr. Garg that Swamiji called Kamal or one of the other girls to bring a white sheet which he spread out in front of him. Then he told Mr. Garg, "Give me your wallet." Swamiji examined its contents, took some money out of the wallet, put it on the sheet and gave the wallet back to Mr. Garg. Swamiji then turned to the other gentleman who had accompanied Mr. Garg and repeated the same performance with his wallet.

Mr. Garg and his friend had some tea and left. I came back and found Swamiji just sitting there with the outspread sheet till about noon. It seems that when the other disciples heard that Swamiji was sitting for bhiksha (alms), they responded generously. Swamiji picked up the sheet and gave it to me. I was shocked to count about 5 million rupees off the white sheet collection. That evening, many more disciples came to offer money to Swamiji. Swamiji refused to take any more money, probably because he had already collected what was needed.

I used to go to the home of Mr.Garg in Dehradun to play cards and would often stay on quite late. Even though Mr. Garg would try to persuade me to go home, I would linger on, pleading that we play just a few more rounds. One night, I left their house around 11:00 p.m. I tend to drive very fast; at least that is what people tell me. I am not quite sure what happened on my way back to Jolly Grant. I felt as if someone forcefully removed my seat, with me in it, out of the car. The seat and I landed on the banks of the Ganges. I don't remember what happened after that. Swamiji phoned Mr. Garg several times that night, asking him to go to Jolly Grant. Mr. Garg was waiting till morning to go. Swamiji again phoned at around 6:00 a.m. and raising his voice scolded Mr. Garg,"Why haven't you gone yet?" Mr. Garg, who had been initiated into a guru mantra by Swamiji, obeyed and left for Jolly Grant right away. When he reached Jolly Grant, he found out that I had met with an accident during the night. The car was very badly damaged. The next day Swamiji came, probably from Delhi. I did not see the car after the accident, because Swamiji gave it away. It was very badly damaged.

I prostate to that guru lineage, which is the origin of eternal knowledge. I prostrate to that Guru... I prostrate to that Guru... I prostrate to that Guru.

Dr. Renu Kapoor

Three Generations Guided and Blessed

Dr. Renu Kapoor

Shrimati Renu Kapoor lives in Kanpur with her mother-in-law and husband, Shri Manoj Kapoor and has two daughters Arima and Garima. Her father was Swami Rama's classmate at Allahabad University. This relationship allowed her to be associated with Swamiji since 1958, when she was only eight years old. She has been inspired not only by Swamiji's lectures and books but also through direct experiential learning. With his grace and guidance, she did her Ph.D. in Child Psychology and her D.Litt. in Indian Psychology (Vedanta and Yoga) which was inspired by his book, *Perennial Psychology of the Bhagavad Gita.* She has been a teacher in a postgraduate college and occasionally does counseling based on Swamiji's teachings. Shrimati Renu treasures every moment spent with Swamiji and feels his presence strongly even today.

My Childhood Memories
of Swami Rama

We were a happy family of four, father, mother, elder sister Maya and me, living in our home, Neelkanth, in Aryanagar, Kanpur. My beloved father, Radhey Shyam Tandon, a devotee of Lord Shiva, was a senior professor of English literature in Christ Church College, Kanpur. Shrimati Kunti, my loving mother, was a simple, religious, sweet-tempered and virtuous housewife.

Swami Rama visited our home for the first time in 1958. Swamiji had been invited by the Jaipurias, a reputed family of Kanpur, to deliver a series of lectures in Kanpur. Dr. Shree Narain Agnihotri, a close friend and classmate of my father at Allahabad University used to attend Swamiji's lectures regularly. One day, after delivering his lecture, Swamiji asked Dr. Agnihotri, "Where is Shyam?" Shyam was the name that my father was known by amongst his close friends. The very next evening, Dr. Agnihotri came to visit my father and told him about this saintly monk who was delivering lectures in the city and who had asked about my father. Dr. Agnihotri urged my father to attend these lectures, but my father refused, stating that he knew nothing about this so-called saint.

Dr. Agnihotri did not give up and came again the next evening to persuade my father to accompany him to the lectures of Swami Rama. My father again refused to go. After Dr. Agnihotri had departed, my mother gently intervened, "If a saint himself wishes to see you, you must go." Reluctantly, my father agreed to attend Swamiji's lectures. At that very moment, we heard the sound of the main gate being opened and moments later, a tall, handsome monk with shaven head, clad in saffron robes and holding a staff, entered our home. My father was overwhelmed at the sight of this imposing personage and spontaneously prostrated at the stranger's feet. The monk, Swami Rama, pulled my father up and hugged him affectionately. It was an amazing, moving sight. It appeared to be the reunion of two long-lost friends. My mother, sister and I did not want to even blink, lest we miss some of this amazing spectacle. Overcome with emotion, my father led Swami Rama to his room, offered him a seat and reverently sat on the ground at his feet. Swamiji announced to my father, "We were classmates at Allahabad University and lived together in the same hostel."

One afternoon, Swamiji came home and agreed to have his lunch with us. Swami Rama was a Dandi Swami. Conforming to tradition, Swamiji would only eat food served by an unmarried maiden. I served him his meal. After his meal, as I was helping him wash his hands, he asked me, "My child, what do you want?" In those days, a lot of emphasis was given to good handwriting. Up to the eighth grade, we were not allowed to use fountain pens. We had to use a pen with a nib which had to be continually dipped in an ink pot. I had seen my father using a fountain pen and had developed the desire for a fountain pen. So when Swamiji asked me what I wanted, I at once replied, "A fountain pen." There was no reaction from Swamiji, but, that very evening, a beautiful, black fountain pen was sent to me. I was overcome with joy.

It was not just an ordinary pen. Through this pen, Swamiji bestowed upon me the blessings of Saraswati, the goddess of learning and wisdom. I realized this forty years later, when I did my Ph.D. in psychology. Ten years later, I was motivated to get a D.Litt. in psychology, all through the grace of Swamiji. I have also taught psychology to postgraduate classes in a reputed college of Kanpur.

My elder sister Maya and I were conversing one day and Maya expressed her hankering for samosas. That evening, as Swamiji stepped into our home, Neelkanth, he asked Maya whether she was thinking of eating samosas. There is another similar incident of the same time period. Maya and I were talking about how we had discussed so many topics with Swamiji, but we had never talked about movies and film stars. We were surprised, when that very night, Swamiji spoke about two very famous film stars of that era, Ashok Kumar and Raj Kapoor. These incidents are testimony to Swamiji's ability to know minds and feelings even across great physical distances.

During his visit to Kanpur in the year 1964, Swamiji stayed at the residence of Dr. K. Sunandabai. He would regularly visit our home at 9:00 p.m. and leave at 4:00 a.m. Swamiji would drive himself in Dr. Sunandabai's green Fiat car. At the approaching sound of his car, I would rush to open the gate and escort Swamiji in. Swamiji, Agnihotriji and my father would be so engrossed in recalling past hostel incidents, other classmates, and their professors that they would lose all sense of time. Night would quietly slip away and when it struck 4:00 a.m., they would be surprised. Sometimes, only Swamiji and my father would talk through the night. My sister and I struggled to stay awake, but often succumbed to slumber. Swamiji would always leave at 4:00 a.m. and Agnihotriji would also go home. Our mother would narrate the events to us in the morning. This routine continued as long as Swamiji stayed in Kanpur. The bond of friendship between Swamiji and my father was deep and unique. Very often, during his stay at Kanpur, Swamiji would go along with my father to Christ Church College. If my father was busy with his class, Swamiji would wait outside for him in his car. When father became free, the two friends would head home to Neelkanth.

Swamiji did not take normal tea which is prepared with a lot of water and a small amount of milk. He preferred "tilk," a term coined by him for tea prepared only with milk, without any water. During his daily visits to our home, my mother, in the beginning, would prepare tilk for Swamiji and whoever else came along with him. Sometimes, there was not enough milk to make tilk for the three or four persons accompanying Swamiji. So, one day, my mother decided that in future she would make tilk only for Swamiji and serve regular tea to the others. As usual, Swamiji arrived in the evening. No sooner had he arrived, than he enquired, "How much milk do I take in tilk?" He then added, "I'll also take regular tea today." My mother was stunned at this decision. She felt guilty thinking that her earlier concerns about the amount of milk required for tilk had led to Swamiji's words and decision. My mother, a simple-hearted, pious lady became depressed and kept cursing herself.

Many years after this incident, I got an opportunity to be with Swamiji in Honesdale, Pennsylvania, in the U.S. We went to his residence to receive his blessings. He gave me the responsibility of preparing tilk. A well-furnished kitchen was attached to his residence. Everything was available there in abundance. He told me to use cardamom and saffron in the preparation of tilk. He then added, "Prepare tilk generously, without considering the cost." I could only smile, being reminded of the years-old incident of my childhood.

My childhood days were fast passing and I was now busy with my school education. Swamiji continued to visit our home whenever he was in Kanpur. We basked in the warmth of his love and affection. We longed for this to never end. I was aware of the fact that Swamiji loved painting. I did not have much talent for painting, but decided to experiment with it as I was eager to win Swamiji's approbation. I purchased a new canvas board and drew the side profile of a woman's face. This was the limit of my creative ability. However, I pretended to continue my contemplation of the painting. An idea occurred to me that while most painters give the face a light shade and paint the hair dark, why should I not do something different. I decided to paint the face black and with my fevered imagination I painted the hair with strokes of many different colors. I was delighted with my creativity and eagerly waited for Swamiji to arrive. The moments ticked away anxiously; at last, Swamiji arrived. No sooner did he arrive, than I, with a delighted heart, presented myself before him. Very humbly I told him that I had made a painting that day which I wanted to show him. Without losing any time, I put my unique creation before him. Casting a look at it, he asked, "What is its caption?" I immediately replied, "A profile." Swamiji remarked, "No, a witch!" And then, by the magic touch of the fingers of his left hand, he made my painting amazingly attractive. In order to encourage me, he agreed to guide me and gave me 10 rupees to purchase painting accessories. The next day, Swamiji asked me to collect some dry sprigs and twigs from the backyard garden. He inspired me to color them in different shades and arranged them artistically in an earthen pot. Thus, Swamiji gave me lessons in art and painting. His careful attention to detail and to even the most insignificant events of life inspired me and helped me in my development.

During his Kanpur stay, Swamiji visited us one night around eight o'clock and asked me to prepare tilk. He took his seat and told our father about having performed Navratri rituals in Vindhyachal from where he had directly come to Kanpur. When I served tilk to Swamiji, I observed a long brilliant white tilak-like mark, about an inch and a half long, on his grand countenance. That night, Swamiji did not stay as usual, through the night, but left soon for the residence of Dr. Sunandabai. After his departure, I mentioned the tilak-like mark I had seen on Swamiji's forehead. Our father said that he too had seen it and had even observed a celestial lustre emanating from it.

We used to share our experiences with Dr. Sunandabai and she would clear our doubts. One day I told her about the tilak-like vision on the forehead of Swamiji and sought an answer to this mystery. Dr. Sunandabai replied, "You are very fortunate. Swamiji has revealed his third eye to you. Lord Shiva came to you, not brandishing his trident (trishool), but in the form of Swamiji." This incident confirmed our conviction that Swamiji is none other than Lord Shiva himself.

As a child, I loved gossip, sports and mimicry. Studies did not attract me. My parents were concerned about my not excelling in studies, and expressed their concern to Swamiji. Dispelling the clouds of their anxiety, he disclosed three secrets:

1. The turning point in her life will come at the age of fourteen.

2. She will herself make her marriage arrangements.

3. She will acquire deep knowledge and high degrees in education.

With the passage of time, I kept getting promoted to higher classes each year. There was a time when I stood among the top four students of my class. In keeping up this position, all other extracurricular activities became of less importance.

My father departed from this material world in September 1975. Before his passing, he had arranged my marriage to Shri Manoj Kapoor and the marriage was to be celebrated in February 1976. The sudden demise of my father disrupted the arrangements of my marriage. Now, there were only two members, my mother and me, in the house. The marriage of my elder sister Maya had already taken place in 1968 to Shri Shiv Nath Tandon and they had settled in Rishikesh. As their daughter Sushmi was very young, Maya could not afford to stay long in Kanpur. She went back to Rishikesh. Ultimately, I had to look after all the arrangements of my marriage. No doubt, I did receive support and guidance from Maya and Shiv Nathji, without which it would not have been possible for me to make all the arrangements appropriately. This was in keeping with Swamiji's prediction regarding my marriage.

Everybody was astonished at the third prediction. But this came to be true in the year 2010, when Kanpur University awarded me a post-doctoral degree (D.Litt.) in psychology. Prior to this, I had received my Ph.D. in psychology in 1985. It may not be out of place to mention that I have the honor of being the first woman recipient of the degree of D.Litt. in psychology in Kanpur University.

I would be most ungrateful if I fail to mention that the study and research for my D.Litt. was crowned with success only because of the grace and compassion of Swamiji. Even the dissertation topic, "Awareness of Self in Framing the Personality," was suggested by Swamiji himself. It is a matter of pride that I received his guidance and co-operation in many ways, directly and indirectly. Virtually, he was my guide, though there is no provision for appointing a guide in Kanpur University. I feel elated and glorified that my research work was done under the graceful guidance of Swamiji, and consider it to be the greatest achievement of my life.

In spite of these regular discussions about hundreds of hostel incidents, my father maintained that he could not recall when exactly Swamiji was his classmate. But, at the same time, he admitted that the incidents which Swamiji recalled were possible only for one who was a witness or a party to these incidents. Swamiji always treated my father as his friend, but my father continued to maintain that he had no memory of any classmate at Allahabad University who resembled Swamiji. My father attributed Swamiji's acceptance of him as a friend to Swamiji's greatness. I do not know what sort of spiritual nexus existed between Swamiji and my father but I was fortunate to have the benefit of their blessed association. I was only eight when the divine presence of Swamiji sanctified our house for the first time. I am 60 now, but the memory of the first darshan of Swamiji is deeply inscribed in my heart and thinking of it still thrills me. This routine ended in 1975, when my father left for his eternal abode.

My father left this mortal world on September 11, 1975. Six months before his demise, Swamiji had invited my father to his ashram, Sadhana Mandir at Rishikesh. On returning from Rishikesh, we noticed a remarkable change in his attitude. He would remark, "I never realized what Swamiji really is. I could not avail of the opportunity of his association. I whiled away the time in mere jokes and jests. He is a divine being." At another time, he would say, "What can I do? It is all his play. I am an ordinary fellow. I did what he wished me to do and saw only what he showed."

Swamiji was in America when my father breathed his last. The late Shri Lakshmi Kant Mishra was with him at that time and later disclosed to us that Swamiji had suddenly declared, "At this time, one of my most intimate friends is departing from this world."

My father, Dr. Radhey Shyam Tandon, was a true devotee of Lord Shiva. He regularly visited the Anandeshwar Temple, Kanpur for worship of his favored deity. He used to recite Shiv Mahimna Stotra in a loud rhythmic tone. Seeing him completely engrossed in this recitation, other devotees would also grow ecstatic. Swamiji was aware of my father's devotion to Lord Shiva. During my father's visit to the Rishikesh ashram, some American disciples were also there. Once, on the prompting of Swamiji, our father performed his worship of Lord Shiva in the ancient Veerbhadra Temple nearby. While he was deeply absorbed in the recitation of the hymn, one of the American devotees recorded it. He must have done it at the instance of Swamiji, but we knew nothing about it. After the death of my father, we received a copy of the cassette from America. This cassette is a precious heirloom of our family.

Swamiji: True Friend, Profound Philosopher and Compassionate Guide

My sister Maya and I were very close to Swamiji. Whenever there was an occasion, he introduced us to his disciples saying, "They are daughters of my friend." Once I was with him when he remembered my elder sister Maya and said, "She has a lot of regard for you." I confirmed it, and said that whenever we had a disagreement, we discussed it, trying to clear things up immediately, without giving room for resentment to build up. Our mutual relations are complementary. Swamiji calmly suggested that reciprocal relations should always be complementary and never competitive.

Swamiji was a recluse, but his worldly dealings were very instructive and inspiring. In the role of a host he was exemplary. The way he received a guest was striking. He never missed the minutest detail in hospitality. He was very attentive to the needs of the guest, to his meals, to the manner of presentation and even to the type of silverware placed. He welcomed the guest whole-heartedly. I myself have observed it in Honesdale, Delhi and at Jolly Grant. He very affectionately insisted on the guest accepting his hospitality. I had the privilege of witnessing such events a number of times. I feel from the very core of my heart, that even a perfect housewife cannot be as skilled in making such arrangements and expressing such deep affection.

Once, my husband Shri Manoj Kapoor and I went to Delhi to see Swamiji, who was staying at his residence in Sarvapriya Vihar. Many important visitors were expected that day. Swamiji gave me the responsibility of arranging for some lig refreshments for these guests. I arranged two or three types of sweets in separate plates. I also put some cut fruits as well as some uncut fruits attractively in separate plates. I did this to the best of my ability. Swamiji entered the room and took a look at my preparations. To my amazement, he put all the sweets in one plate, all the fruits in another big plate and rearranged the plates in a very artistic manner. His presentation was so attractive that it would draw the attention of the visitor and tempt him to taste all the items offered.

After making all the arrangements Swamiji told me, "Always bear in mind that whenever you are serving meals to anyone, serve generously, offering as many items as possible. Keep serving till the guest says, 'I am full, that's enough!' Only in eating does one attain fulfillment and contentment. Give a man anything else, there will always remain some iota of dissatisfaction." Swamiji thus made me aware of the importance of serving food aesthetically and generously.

The mind and feelings of his disciples and followers were always within Swamiji's ambit. Distance was no hurdle. Their thoughts and sentiments were always in his ken. I too have experienced it. Once, without planning, Manoj and I reached Delhi for his darshan. He was staying at the India International Center. Reaching there, we gently knocked on his door. Within a few moments, he himself partially opened the door, peeped out, blessed us and without asking us to come in and sit down said, "Now go back." We reached the railway station on our journey back to

Kanpur. With the sounds of the moving train, this thought kept hammering upon my mind, "Probably, we are neither of any use to Swamiji nor can we be of any service to him. Then, why should he ask us to stay or to sit with him?" This thought agitated me and I considered myself worthless.

Time passed. A few days after this incident, I got an opportunity to go to Rishikesh. Swamiji was at the ashram. He got word of my arrival and was kind enough to send through Kamal his blessings, and an invitation for me to come to his room. I literally rushed there and presented myself before him. Swamiji was sitting on the terrace outside his room. He asked me to sit down and inquired after my welfare. We talked about a number of topics. At that time, I was studying a book on Tantra Vidya. It was in the nature of a novel. It had affected my approach to my surroundings and infused in me negative thoughts. I discussed this matter with Swamiji. He listened to me very attentively and then asked, "Do you not read my books?" I had nothing more to say that day. I felt relieved. All of this conversation took about one and a half hours. I, of my own accord, rose from my seat, bowed in reverence before him, intending to leave. He did not ask me to leave. He only said, "Do you still feel that Swamiji does not ask you to sit down?" I immediately recalled the Delhi incident and could not but smile. This incident has assured me that Swamiji pays attention to even the most insignificant desires of common folk like me and fulfils them.

It was 1988. I and my family were in Minneapolis, U.S.A. with my elder sister Maya. Swamiji was in town and asked Maya to make arrangements for kirtan at her place that evening. Without losing any time, Maya contacted one of her acquaintances and made arrangements for tabla and harmonium. The kirtan started in the evening. Swamiji sang his favorite devotional song "Radha Madhava", and prompted us to join him. We were lost in the rapture of the divine song and wished to remain immersed in the music. Even though we were not very proficient in singing, we chimed in for some time with Swamiji. He tolerated us for a few minutes; then putting aside the harmonium, he said, "If I continue to sing with you any longer, it will damage my harmony and rhythm." It was his way of dispelling the monotony and making the atmosphere light and congenial.

My mother had also accompanied us to Minneapolis. One fine day, Swamiji graced us by his dignified presence. It was the Ganga Dussehra that day. Having performed her worship, my mother gave us a little Gangajal (Ganga water) on our palms to sip. She had brought it with her from Kanpur. Swamiji also sipped the holy water. He then told my mother, "I have decided to establish a hospital in India. Offer your worship by doing one rosary every day for the accomplishment of my resolve." My mother sincerely acted in accordance with his wish, every day without fail, till her last breath in the year 2000.

Swamiji had the divine ability to ward off any bodily ailment. Once my mother contracted herpes, a very painful disease. According to physicians, recovery from it takes almost six long months. But, by the grace of Swamiji, my mother got freedom from this distress within only three days.

As soon as my father knew that mother was in the grip of herpes, he went to Dr. M. K. Mitra, a renowned Homeopath of Kanpur, a brother disciple of Swamiji. Dr. Mitra received a call from Swamiji at the same time. When Swamiji learnt that my father was there, he spoke to him and inquired about the reason for his visit to the doctor. My father told Swamiji the details of my mother's ailment. Swamiji again spoke to Dr. Mitra and suggested a homeopathic remedy which he prescribed for my mother. She took the medicine as instructed and, strikingly, within three days, all symptoms of the disease disappeared. The doctor who had diagnosed herpes was amazed when he heard of my mother's miraculous recovery.

Later on, the mystery was revealed. Swamiji was staying with Dr. Sunandabai then. Revealing the secret, she told us that Swamiji too had taken one dose of the same medicine which he had suggested to Dr. Mitra for my mother. How kind he had been to us! In this way, he showered his blessings on our family. I have been fortunate to receive guidance from him, directly and indirectly. Even after he shed his mortal coil, he has very kindly continued to bless and guide me.

Swamiji Guides my Studies
in Psychology

Psychology is my favorite field of study. I did postgraduation in this subject and also taught postgraduate classes. I did research in this very subject for which I was awarded the degree of Ph.D. The psychology which is studied in India has its source in western philosophy. In the West, the initial phase of the study of psychology was centered on mind and soul, but soon its emphasis was changed to the study of human behavior. The subtle study and detailed analysis of soul is much less in western philosophy compared to the traditions of Indian philosophy. Consequently, modern psychology does not give importance to study of the soul.

During my teaching career, I seriously studied the books of Swamiji and philosophical topics described therein, namely, yoga, Vedanta, Upanishads and also other good books and scriptures in addition to an intensive study of my subject. This had become my daily routine. With the passage of time, I started tracing the sources of psychology in Indian philosophy. I discovered a deep ocean of relevant matter there. All at once, an idea sprouted in my mind: "Why should I not do my research work on Indian psychology?" In continuation of this chain of thought, it instantaneously flashed upon my mind that I must put this matter before Swamiji. I immediately contacted him on the phone. He was in Delhi at that time. I was overwhelmed when he himself received the call. I apprised him of my intention to study the sources of psychology in Indian philosophy. At that time, I had just finished the study of Swamiji's book, *Perennial Psychology of the Bhagavad Gita.* I was deeply impressed by the Gita and its unique commentary by Swamiji. The Gita preaches disinterested action. It also teaches that the effect of every action is inevitable, but its time and nature should not be the concern of the doer. He should leave it to the Supreme Self. On the other hand, western conception of modern psychology is that every action has its reaction. It may be in the form of reward or punishment. This uncertainty begets tension. I conveyed the findings of my study to Swamiji without pausing to take a breath. I concluded my talk with the words. "If I get your permission, I would like to do postdoctoral research (D.Litt.) on this subject alone." In his calm tone, he made a very brief reply, "All right. Meet Ajay Swami. He is staying at Sadhana Mandir, Rishikesh. I am also reaching there." My happiness knew no bounds. Arrangements for the journey were made immediately. The very next day, I with my husband Manoj reached the ashram.

Ajay Swami (original name Allen Weinstock) was a clinical psychologist from America. Besides being an eminent scholar of modern psychology, he had a deep and wide knowledge of Indian philosophy as well. He very patiently listened to me, questioned and counter-questioned me in between, gave suggestions and also expressed his opinion. Consequently, the scope of the treatise and its main points became clear.

That night we stayed in the ashram. Very early, the next morning, there was some commotion. On coming out of the room, we learnt that Swamiji had arrived. We went to pay our respects to him. We also apprised him of our meeting with Ajay Swami. He directed us to go on to Jolly Grant.

We reached Jolly Grant at the appointed time and informed Swamiji about our discussions with Ajay Swami and the conclusions drawn. He heard me attentively and blessed me with his words, "Start your work. I'll guide you." With these encouraging words of benediction, I came out of his room. I was extremely happy.

After coming back to Kanpur, I started my perusal of Indian philosophy from the point of view of psychology, prepared an outline of the research work and wrote a general introduction of the proposed treatise. I could not resist the temptation of presenting it before Swamiji as early as possible. Without waiting for the typed copy, I sent the manuscript to Swamiji through Malini Srivastava who was visiting Kanpur at that time and was returning to Jolly Grant.

It was my heartfelt desire that Swamiji should go through my manuscript. Malini helped me in this matter and informed me that she had put the papers in his bag. After a few days, I received two directions through her: One, that my handwriting was very bad and needed improvement, and secondly, that the material was very scattered and needed to be well knit.

Regarding the research work, I had to frequently visit Swamiji, either in Delhi or at Jolly Grant. During this period I had a few astonishing experiences. I would like to share some of these experiences with you.

My research work was progressing rapidly. Notes were being prepared but the topic was yet to be decided. When I decided on a topic, the very next moment, my own reasoning would find grounds to reject it. In this state of uncertainty, I decided to take refuge at the feet of Swamiji in Jolly Grant. Here I would like to share with the readers that whenever I approached Swamiji with any of my problems, the first inquiry he made was always directly related to my problem. Every time he discussed the main points of my research. I used to listen to him and take detailed notes. Keeping all this in mind, I made arrangements for a tape recorder.

The first question which he asked was pertaining to my problem: "What is the topic?" I replied with hesitation, "Swamiji, I have not been able to decide on a topic as yet." Snubbing me, he said, "Six months have passed and you have not chosen a topic." The next moment he said, "Write, 'Awareness of Self in Framing the Personality.'" I noted it down. I was assured that every word of the conversation was being recorded. I took his leave and came out of his room. I was pleased that Swamiji had himself selected the topic and it had been recorded also.

On reaching my room in Nanak Sarai, I immediately rewound the tape, in order to hear the voice of Swamiji with patience and concentration. I played the tape. But, lo, what happened? There was nothing on the tape except what he had instructed concerning the topic: "Write, 'Awareness of Self in framing the personality.'" The rest of the cassette was blank. Only my notes were available to me.

There was another experience worth noting. Reading and writing were going on simultaneously. But the mind was unsteady. The basis of the thesis was Self and I was finding myself incompetent to describe it. I had no realization of Self. While there was no hindrance in reading, cogitation and meditation, on account of this deficiency, writing had been interrupted. One night, immersed in these thoughts, I fell asleep. All of a sudden, I felt someone was calling me in a grim and sober voice. He said, "Get up. Write it." Baffled, I got up at once, switched the light on, took pen and paper and sat down to write. I went on writing about a page on Self, as if I was taking a dictation. In the end I was asked to write the conclusion of my research, "Self is the very basis of life, and personality is the result of its awareness." This hypothesis formed the foundation of my thesis.

Swamiji's style of explaining obscure subjects was unique. Prior to making clear the mystery of the esoteric doctrine of philosophy, he would give the person a direct example of the same, and then, if necessary, he would explain the doctrinal aspect.

The central theme of my thesis was Vedanta. I had acquired academic knowledge of the theoretical aspects of Vedanta but its emotional realization was lacking. An occurrence of that time gave me its practical experience. One day a cat died in my room. Gradually it started stinking. I requested the sweepers to throw it out but they refused. The bad smell was increasing and this was making me nauseous. Till now, I was looking at the cat as a dead animal only. Suddenly, there was a flash. An idea sprang into my mind: "Research work on Oneness, . . . dead cat is a low animal . . . such dualistic behavior!" Maybe Swamiji himself had forced this thought upon me. I shook off negative thoughts then and there. I picked up the carcass, took it to the dust bin away from the house and dumped it there. Thus, Swamiji had made me aware of the practical aspect of the Vedantic concept of the presence of the omnipresent Brahman in all living beings, irrespective of species.

Once, I had expressed my doubt before Swamiji that social inequality obstructs advait darshan (vision of oneness) becoming the basis of social interactions. Society is concerned with differences of caste and creed, haves and have-nots, male and female, etc. Swamiji explained that the feeling of oneness obviates all sorts of negative thoughts, while existence of emotions of duality gives rise to delusion and distinction. Hence, such feelings are due to ignorance.

It was Swamiji's mission to make the mystery of life clear in very simple and lucid language. It is my conviction that by observing his behavior, interactions and pithy statements, one could make one's life fruitful. Once, by chance, I was fortunate to be alone with Swamiji. Taking advantage of the opportunity, I wanted to ask him how we should deal with others. Making my intention clear, I said, "Swamiji, it is the way of the world today that a humble person is taken to be either inferior or impoverished. Then, to what degree should one practice humility?" He explained with usual calm, "Always bear in mind that you are meek only before that part of the Almighty which is within a person and not to the worldly individual. Therefore, always be submissive and respectful to other people." On another occasion, I sought his opinion on the style of writing, whether it should be informative or suggestive. He instantly stated that it should always be informative, never suggestive.

At Kanpur University, there is no formal provision for a research guide for postdoctoral research work. But I admit in my heart of hearts, that if at all my research work was progressing, it was possible only due to the guidance of Swamiji. Perhaps this acceptance was pretentious, and somewhere, vanity was lurking. In some corner of my heart there was a strong feeling that I of my own accord was elaborating such a complicated subject that included advait philosophy and the practical aspects of ashtanga yoga for the realization of Swa (Self).

During my stay at Jolly Grant, Swamiji wanted to know who my guide was. I was already puffed up with ego. So my immediate reply was, "Swamiji, there is no provision for a guide." As soon as I came out of his room, I became guilt ridden and was filled with deep remorse. What had I blurted out? I had been telling everyone that Swamiji himself was guiding me. Perhaps I was just prattling. That must be my ego and definitely not self-confidence.

I came back to Kanpur. After some time, I again got an opportunity to go to Jolly Grant. I straightway went to Swamiji's residence. He was strolling in the veranda. Seeing me, he asked, "Who is your guide?" I promptly replied, "Swamiji, none but you." A smile lit up his face. I too had a smile. Now I was confident. Swamiji had his unique style of instruction and redemption from negative thinking.

My synopsis was approved by the University in April 1996. With a happy heart and full of zeal, I seriously and sincerely started writing regularly and systematically. I decided that initially a brief outline of every chapter should be prepared, after which each chapter could be elaborated on the basis of this outline. It took nine or ten days to write up a brief summary of all seven chapters of the thesis. I used to be glued to my chair at the table from nine in the morning till nine or ten in the evening. I took breaks only for meals or for some unavoidable event. I had a strong urge or compulsion from within and relaxation was beyond my power. There was a flood of thoughts and I was only penning them down automatically. Such a long sitting every day caused swelling in my feet. The members of my family did not appreciate my impatience. But I was helpless. I was trying hard to keep up with this powerful flood of thoughts. Thus I succeeded in preparing an outline of the thesis. Strange! I did not know from where and how I could gather so much physical and mental energy to complete this task.

On reaching Jolly Grant on the occasion of Janmashtami, I came to know that Swamiji was not maintaining good health. I went to his room and admitted, "Swamiji, you dispatch very powerful thoughts, but my capacity fails to express them appropriately." He had already assured me that he would help me in getting the research work done. Therefore, in response to my admission, he consoled me saying, "I'll get it done too."

In due course, my thesis was complete. But by then Swamiji's immortal soul had broken free from the bonds of the mortal gross body. The thesis had been submitted to the University for review. For want of some scholarly experts, the review process was getting delayed. It was making me impatient and increasing my anxiety about the result. I soothed myself to maintain self-confidence. When Swamiji himself had deigned to guide me, the result had to be positive. Inspite of all this, human weakness was at its play. One day, I heard Swamiji's voice, "Don't get disturbed. You will get the degree in due course of time. It is only a mental ornament. Whatever you have written or realized, practice that."

Even today, with open heart and with deep gratitude I admit that writing of the thesis is his greatest boon to me.

Inauguration of the
Medical College
HIHT, Jolly Grant

Swamiji was deft in converting hardships into opportunities for learning and growth. I too had a chance to realize this. This incident is related to the inauguration of the medical college. I had an earnest desire to witness this inaugural function but there was no point in going to Jolly Grant without proper information of the planned program.

One day I received an invitation card dispatched by HIHT. On opening it I found an invitation for the inauguration of the medical college. I was greatly delighted. But my delight was shortlived when I realized that the program was to take place just two days later. Despite this, I decided to proceed to Jolly Grant with my older daughter Arima to participate in the function. No train reservation was readily available. I contacted my travel agent to get two berths reserved for Haridwar that very night, either from Kanpur or via Lucknow. By evening, the travel agent expressed his inability to get us train reservations. Now, the only alternative was to travel by bus.

Early the next morning, around 4:00 a.m., our bus left Kanpur. The journey was to be accomplished in three phases. In the first phase, we had to go from Kanpur to Bareilly, then from Bareilly to Haridwar and finally from Haridwar to Jolly Grant. By eleven o'clock we were at Bareilly. From there we proceeded to Haridwar by another bus. After covering a distance of 40 km., the bus broke down. It made me restless. After some time, it started moving again. But, now its speed was way below normal. Somehow or other the bus reached Moradabad by evening. There, we learnt that it would be night by the time the bus reached Haridwar. We then had to travel further, from Haridwar to Jolly Grant. The thought of the two of us, mother and daughter, finding shelter for the night in an unfamiliar city disturbed me. It was a monstrous problem, and time was fleeting fast. Our target was to reach the inaugural function in time. So we immediately decided to continue the remaining journey by train. If the train were late, we could spend the night in the railway retiring room.

With this decision, both us reached the railway station at Moradabad. There we received information that a passenger train on the Saharanpur-Roorkee route was about to leave and a superfast train would follow an hour later. We had to alight at Roorkee. The choice was between these two trains. We preferred to travel by the superfast train. I phoned one of my acquaintances in Roorkee to meet us at the railway station. He very kindly agreed to receive us. There was an announcement that the superfast train was running late, so we purchased tickets and boarded the passenger train. The passenger train was moving at its usual slow speed. After crossing two or three flag stations it stopped at a small station. It remained there a long time. We came to know that its engine had failed. We heard that another engine was being called to drag it. The process could take three hours or more. A problem had arisen again. Now what should be done? In discussions with fellow passengers, it became clear that the superfast train from Moradabad was due to arrive but that it would stop at this station for only three minutes. One of the fellow travelers, probably a

railway employee, consoled me saying that I should
not worry. He would help me in changing trains and
would also speak to the conductor for seats. The train
arrived at eleven o'clock at night and this gentleman,
very kindly helped Arima and me to shift to the other
train comfortably.

We were faced with a chain of problems. When
one problem was resolved, another reared its head. As
there was no illumination on stations along the way,
it was very difficult to know which station was next.
The train had its stop at Roorkee for only two to three
minutes. I was again disturbed. When I discussed my
problem with a fellow passenger, he said that it was no
problem. He would alert me before hand. He too had
to get down at Roorkee. Now I was able to relax. The
train reached Roorkee at about two in the morning.
My family friend was waiting on the platform. We
stayed at his place for the rest of the night and reached
Haridwar by bus at seven that morning.

Now the last phase of the journey remained. The
inaugural function was to commence at nine o'clock.
Knowing Swamiji's penchant for punctuality, I knew
that it would not be delayed for any reason. For this
reason, we preferred to take an autorickshaw for the
last leg of the journey. There was an ongoing agitation
for creating Uttarakhand as an independent state,
rather than being part of Uttar Pradesh. The people
of Uttarakhand were strongly opposed to the visit of
the Prime Minister, P. V. Narasimha Rao, who was
coming to inaugurate the medical college. On account
of the agitation, no auto driver was willing to go to
Jolly Grant. We were now faced with a new problem.
Meanwhile a driver approached me, inquired about
my destination, and on hearing the name Jolly Grant,
readily agreed to take us there. We resumed our
journey. After travelling some distance, the driver

picked up another person on the way who sat beside the driver. I was afraid. Suddenly, the stranger asked me if I was going to the function of the Baba. My answer was in the affirmative.

The autodriver was following a short cut. Only half an hour was left for the commencement of the program. I was growing increasingly anxious and restless. I requested the driver to speed up the autorickshaw. The stranger advised me to have patience. Now, I had no alternative but to accede to his advice.

As soon as we reached the Bhaniawala junction of three roads, another hurdle was waiting for us. The Prime Minister was going to attend the program. Therefore, the security measures were very tight and the road traffic was being controlled. For reasons of security, our auto was stopped. I explained my position to the senior police officer on duty there and told him that on account of luggage, it would not be possible for me to travel three to four km. on foot. I showed him the invitation card for the inaugural function and told him that we had come all the way from Kanpur just to attend this function. Seeing the invitation card, the officer said, "Showing this card, take your vehicle onward. Nobody will stop you." I was not stopped even at the gate of HIHT and my auto took me straight to the main pandal which was reserved for the VVIPs. It was just nine o' clock, the scheduled time for the function.

I turned and noticed that Swamiji was coming to the pandal dressed in his favourite maroon gown. I bowed to him from where I was. He was wearing dark glasses, so I could not tell if he had seen me. But I had the satisfaction of being there just in time.

After a while, when my restlessness had calmed down, I pondered over the entire experience. I realized that I had not reached there, but had actually been called. I was simply being guided by the will of Swamiji. All the hurdles on the way had been removed by none other than his agents, unknown to me. With unflinching faith in him, all my efforts had been directed towards only one goal, which was to reach the venue at the right time.

After the closing of the function, when I met Swamiji, he said affectionately, "I am pleased that you and Arima have come." I narrated to him all that had happened on the way. In reaction to it, a loving smile played on his face. I was overwhelmed with joy.

On reconsidering these incidents, I felt that we, mother and daughter, were driven by our desire to attend the function. Thinking of how much trouble Swamiji might have faced in the fulfillment of our desire, I grew sad.

It is a fact that the train of desires is endless. They keep on coming, one after the other. But we should always introspect whether these desires are essential and practical. When we find ourselves incapable of fulfilling them, we turn to our guru, the spiritual guide. Here too, we must ponder whether our invoking the guru would inconvenience the guru. A true disciple always avoids disturbing the guru. The teachings of all the great saints have shown us how to escape from such situations. They have taught that we should attenuate our desires by contemplation and discipline and should ultimately try to become desireless.

Swamiji's Passage into the Light

By chance, I happened to visit Jolly Grant in 1996.
Swamiji was there. He had been sick but now was in
better health. I was bewildered at the news, because
my presumption was that nothing could happen
against his will. Why would he want to be sick?

After paying my respects to him, I sat down and
during the course of general talk, out of curiosity, I
put a question regarding his health, "How long will it
continue?" With his natural smile, he raised his forefinger, in reply to my question. I was astonished and
in order to quench my anxiety, I again asked, "One
year?" He shook his head in disagreement, and said,
"One month." After this pleasant short meeting, I
returned to Kanpur.

My elder daughter Arima was a student of B.Com.
in Dehradun, under the guardianship of Swamiji. She
was fortunate enough to stay with Swamiji on Sundays
and other holidays. Before Deepavali, Arima sought
his permission to go to Kanpur. He wanted to know
the reason. Arima referred to the occasion of Deepavali
and said that she also had to bring woollen clothes for
the coming winter. In his grave and cryptic manner,
Swamiji said, "I do not detain a person intending to
go, but will your mother not come to see me?" Arima
conveyed this information to me over the phone.

My sister Maya informed me from Minneapolis
that my brother-in-law, Shri Shiv Nath Tandon was

reaching Jolly Grant to see Swamiji on the occasion
of Deepavali. She sincerely wished that I should also
reach there at that time. On my inquiry about this
unexpected program, she said, "Do not try to know
the reason, I cannot tell you."

Maya's message made me restless. A host of
questions flooded my heart. Why was my brother-in-
law not celebrating Deepavali at home? Swamiji could
not be indisposed, because it was my firm conviction
that his health depended on his own sweet will. Even
so, I decided to reach Jolly Grant as soon as possible.
Consequently, after offering worship on Deepavali, I
left for Jolly Grant the very next day, the Pratipada
day, against Indian tradition. I had already obtained
the consent and co-operation of the members of my
family.

The train took me to Haridwar at the right time.
Shiv Nathji, his daughter Mandavi, my daughter
Arima, and Malini were waiting for me on the platform.
A vehicle of the Himalayan Institute was also there. It
had come to fetch somebody else who had not been
able to come. We availed of the opportunity that had
fortuitously presented itself.

Having arranged our stay at Nanak Sarai, we
immediately proceeded towards Swamiji's residence.
On the way, we met Maithili. In response to my
question, "How is Swamiji?" she kept silent. Even
then, I was not very worried about Swamiji's health
on account of my confidence in his willpower. I could
not have his darshan that afternoon. He allowed
everybody to pay a visit in the evening. Those who
were waiting went to have his darshan one by one,
and he blessed everyone by putting his hand on their
head. Having received his blessings, we came out and
stood under a tree beside his apartment.

Later that evening, Swamiji came out of his apartment. He took the support of Dr. Singhal with one of his arms and raised the other in search of another shoulder. Seeing this, I gave an indication to my brother-in-law, Shiv Nathji, who immediately ran to Swamiji who placed the other hand on his head and moved towards his car. On the way, his compassion caught sight of me too. I expressed my obeisance to him from a distance, and he raised both of his hands in a gesture of blessing. Simultaneously, he gave me a signal of "one" by raising his index finger. I thought he was stopping me, but that was not his indication.

The following day, Swamiji did not come out of his room. Late in the evening, I reached his apartment on my own. Getting no signal to go in, I sat down on the stairs outside and started crying like a child, because by now, his condition had become quite clear. Sitting there in the throes of my emotions, I was praying to Swamiji to give me an opportunity to serve him. Having prayed for about an hour, I went back to my room. A strange quiet was pervading the surroundings. I came across a number of people, but nobody was talking to anyone. All were silent, lost in their own thoughts. When at about 11:30 that night, we received a message to go to the apartment, the mystery of Swamiji's index finger was revealed.

The body of Swamiji, wrapped in his well known maroon gown, was placed on the bed. Some of the members of the guru family were in the apartment and some were standing outside, stunned. Kamal asked me to go sit in the room where his body was placed. From midnight till morning, I remained seated there, quite still. A number of diverse thoughts continued to rise in my mind. The reel of my experiences with Swamiji, from his first visit to our home in 1958 till the previous day, was playing on the screen of my mind.

I was continuously looking at his physical body. I perceived that the fingers of both his hands were in the posture of japa, his eyes were partially closed and the great sage was looking after his physical body himself. The thought that Swamiji was alive and asleep, was intermittently arising in the mind. I was lost in these thoughts; time moved on undeterred and it was now sunrise.

In the morning, Swamiji's mortal remains were placed in the outer room of his apartment, for people to have his last darshan. The unbroken flow of his devotees, disciples and followers continued throughout the day. The visitors included all, common folk as well as VVIPs. The next morning, Swamiji's body was kept on a raised platform between his apartment and the Combined Therapy building. Thousands of devotees paid their tributes with handfuls of flowers and tear-filled eyes.

His body was taken to Haridwar for cremation in the afternoon. I was also asked to take part in the funeral rites. According to Indian tradition, women do not go to the cremation ground. Swamiji was the friend of my father and all of my family regarded him not only as the head of the family but also as the soul of the family. So I refrained from going to the funeral ground. Another thought crept into my mind, "Swamiji is my guru, and the guru is immortal. Then, why should I participate in the final journey of his mortal body?" These thoughts prevented me from attending his last rites.

Did Swamiji Attend His Own Shodashi Rite?

Around nine o'clock, on the last night of Swamiji's worldly life, I was sitting on the stairs beside his apartment. I was praying to him that I too wanted to serve him, beseeching him to provide me time and an opportunity to serve him. But my yearning remained unfulfilled, as that very night, at about eleven o'clock, Gurudev escaped the mortal cage. The whole campus was plunged in sorrow.

The Guru is Brahman and is immortal and imperishable. Like Brahman, he also is omnipresent. So I felt assured that I would have his darshan again, even if only once. But would it be possible for me to recognize him in his new form and shape? It was the occasion of Swamiji's Shodashi, the sixteenth day after his passing. I was lost in these very thoughts. There was a huge program in Jolly Grant. Elaborate arrangements were made for havan and bhandara. A number of saints and sages had come from far off places to take part in this program. Thousands of men and women, old and young had come from their native places and from abroad.

It was my firm belief that our gurudev would come on this occasion in one form or another. I shared this view with a few members of our guru family. I requested them to be on the alert and to maintain secrecy. They agreed with me.

We were deeply anxious to see Gurudev, but the problem was, how to recognize him? In the depth of my heart, a continuous prayer to him was going on, that he himself should indicate his presence; otherwise it would be beyond the power of our worldly senses to recognize him. With this prayer in my heart, I was sitting in a corner of the pandal. Both my daughters, Arima and Garima were with me. After the final offerings into the havan, I become more vigilant. My eager eyes were scanning the gathering, looking for Gurudev in an unknown body. All of a sudden, my eyes fell upon a sage of average frame with a long grey beard, wearing pants and a dusty shirt and jacket, a band tied around his head. Somehow, I felt attracted to this dignified personality. I at once alerted Arima and Garima and headed towards this dignified and attractive sage. Approaching him and addressing him as Swamiji, I paid my regards and bowed respectfully. The Mahatmaji (I addressed the sage with this word, meaning great soul) looked at me with his natural penetrating eyes and said, "Recognize God."

Subsequently, pointing at his headband he said, "Open this band and tie it again." While I was executing his command, he asked me, "Where has your mind been all this while?" I replied, "I don't know; I could not concentrate even during the havan." He said, "All right." After getting the headband tied, he said to me, "Bring some water for me. All are thirsty." (I could not comprehend the sense of "all" at that time.) I offered Mahatmaji several glasses of water one after another. Each time, he covered the glass with a cloth, made the gesture of drinking water, and put the emptied glass aside. I noticed something most astonishing. The glasses were getting empty, but the covering cloth did not get wet!

Having quenched his thirst with 17 to 18 glasses of water, Mahatmaji desired to go to the pandal of the bhandara. The arrangement for the general feast was made near the pandal where the havan was conducted. While going in that direction, he put one of his hands on my shoulder and the other on that of Arima. On the way, while passing in front of Swamiji's apartment, he said suddenly, "Swami Rama is in me at present, but don't disclose it to anyone else. If you do, people will start thrashing both you and me." By now we had reached the place of bhandara. Mahatmaji sat down on the ground and asked me to make arrangements for his food. By this time, I was fully convinced that reverend Swamiji himself was with us in the form of this person.

There was a newspaper lying on the ground, where my daughters and I were sitting with Mahatmaji. A general invitation of Swamiji's Shodashi with his portrait was published prominently. Pointing towards the advertisement, Arima asked, "Who is he?" Mahatmaji replied, "Whatever is going on here is very much his celebration." Out of our eagerness and ignorance we were trying to confirm that Mahatmaji himself was the embodiment of Swamiji.

While sitting at the bhandara site, Mahatmaji started kirtan and advised us to do kirtan adding that it would attract the holy souls in the vicinity to gather around us. (Prompted by this statement, kirtan of the devotional songs sung by Swamiji on cassette still continues at my residence every Thursday.)

Mahatmaji was sitting happily on the ground near the bhandara. I had called Malini to come there. Maithili too was with us. Mahatmaji himself had asked us to call out to her. Arima, Malini and Mathili had the privilege of having Swamiji's special favor and compassion. He spoke to them in different ways.

All three admitted that what he talked about were known only to them and Swami Rama. They were overwhelmed upon conversing with the Mahatma.

After having his meal, Mahatmaji asked us to call Dr. A. P. Singh, who had been put in charge of the bhandara arrangements. The Mahatmaji said to him in English, "The whole of India will feel proud of you."

Now, Mahatmaji expressed a desire to go to the place where I was staying. I proceeded with him to Nanak Sarai. Again he took the support of Arima's and my shoulders. I felt that he had difficulty in movement. Moving slowly, we reached Nanak Sarai. He sat down and took off his jacket. He took out several hundred rupee notes from each pocket and placed them before me saying, "They will take away my money." (I did not understand what he meant.) Mahatmaji gave Rs. 16.75 to Garima with the words, "Go and buy a book for yourself." There was an old lady sweeper of the hospital standing nearby. Mahatmaji gave her some money and told her to fetch some tea for him.

With the approach of the evening, some thoughts started agitating me. Chiefly two types of feelings were rising up in my mind. First, was I committing some sentimental folly overcome by the flood of emotions? Second, if he was really Gurudev, I was incapable of giving him proper service. In this state of indecisiveness, I said to Mahatmaji, "Now I am not in a position to serve you any further. So kindly leave for your destination." Mahatmaji said to Arima, "Your mother wants to get rid of me." At the same time, he asked me to take him to the station.

In order to take him to the station, I requested several persons to arrange a vehicle. But on account of people being busy with the program, this could not be done. Mahatmaji had difficulty in walking and the railway station was quite far away, I saw Dr. A. P. Singh coming. I ran to him and told him about the situation, requesting him to make some arrangement. A pickup van of the Institute was standing there. Mahatmaji authoritatively called it and took the seat beside the driver, giving me some room to sit down beside him. (I had wished, sometime in the past, to travel sitting beside Swamiji.) On the way to the station I asked him, "Is what I am thinking and comprehending correct?" He replied, "Do you still have doubts? I will visit you in Kanpur, too." I had not told Mahatmaji that I belonged to Kanpur.

On reaching the Doiwala railway station, I purchased a ticket to Dehradun for just Rs. 17. (Mahatmaji had given Garima Rs. 16.75 for a book.) The train was not at the platform, but was standing on the middle track. Thinking that Mahatmaji had trouble walking, I tried to find some way to take him to the train. In the meantime, Mahatmaji rushed forth and jumping like a young man boarded the train. It was hard to believe that he was the same Mahatmaji who was not able to walk properly in Jolly Grant, but could now enter the train compartment with so much energy. It was six o'clock in the evening. Standing on the platform, I was waiting for the departure of the train. The train started moving and the Mahatmaji, raising both hands, blessed us and bade us farewell.

Prior to this, I had requested Mahatmaji to write a few words in my diary. He said, "I will dictate, you write." He dictated, "The Lord shall protect us twenty-four hours of the day from the temptation of luxuries. He is all in all, and He is much closer to us. We should be watchful that we walk on the path of perfection and truth." Mahatmaji then signed my diary.

This unprecedented incident made it clear to me that Gurudev had accepted my prayer to provide me an opportunity to serve and had fulfilled that unfulfilled desire. Even after being freed from the bonds of the mortal body, Gurudev guides his devotees and disciples in one way or another. In compliance with the advice given by Mahatmaji, kirtan is continuing at my residence for the last 14 years. During these kirtan sessions, we have had some strange, unique, and even celestial experiences. The secret has also been disclosed that it is not necessary for the guru to appear in his own form. He may come in any form.

Dr. Sunandabai: a Dedicated and Devoted Disciple

The name of Dr. Sunandabai is well known to almost all guru brothers and sisters. She was a dedicated gynecologist of repute who had retired as the head of the department of gynecology in GSVM Medical College, Kanpur. She was a strict disciplinarian who had never married and had made Kanpur in the north her home, even though she was originally from South India. As far as I know, Swamiji always stayed at her home. She did not have a feeling of ownership even for her own home. She always held that everything belonged to Swamiji and she owned nothing. She was whole heartedly devoted and dedicated to Swamiji and was a true disciple. I am one of those fortunate persons upon whom she has showered her affection profusely.

Outspokenness was one of the attributes of Dr. Sunandabai. Sometimes she was so blunt that it appeared shocking to the listener. She accepted gifts from no one. She would return gifts, telling the giver that she lived alone and there was none else in the house to use the gift. One day, she herself recounted that Swamiji had once said to her, "You speak very bitter truths. It is violence of speech." She frankly responded, "You are my master. You alone can reform me."

Dr. Sunandabai had total self-control and discipline. The second floor of her house was reserved for Swamiji. When Swamiji stayed there, she would unfailingly go to him once in the morning, to pay her respects to him (charan-sparsha). After this, she would only go to him if he called for her. She was most uncompromising in her values. Whenever she was asked about her welfare, her uniform reply was, "Respected Swamiji is at the helm of my boat. Therefore, I am all right."

Swamiji's physical disappearance from this temporal world had created a void in our lives. We began to prefer the company of only those persons who loved to talk about him and narrate their reminiscences of him. This preference drove me towards Dr. Sunandabai. One day, she wished to see my mother. On October 15, 1997, I went to see her with my mother. We had a long talk about Swamiji that day. She appeared to be in good health then.

Now, I would like to share my memories of the last days of Dr. Sunandabai. I bear witness to those days. On the evening of October 18, 1997, I was informed about a sudden deterioration in her health. The next day, October 19, I went to see her with my husband Manoj. On receiving information of our arrival, she came out of her room with the support of her domestic help Udai Singh and his wife Narayani. She was standing erect, Udai Singh and Narayani were behind her, but she looked very pale. We were meeting again after an interval of only three days. But her condition suggested to us that she was preparing for her final journey. She came and sat down on the sofa and put a direct question to me, "Who informed you?" Without giving me a chance to speak, she herself replied, "Bhadauriyaji might have told you." She just did not like to talk about herself. Therefore, I simply smiled at her question and her own answer. She insisted upon our having something to eat. It was her temperament that she would not let anyone leave her home without partaking of some food. It was the auspicious day of Karvachauth. So, I was observing a fast. But Manoj had to honor her wish. I told her, "If you permit, we can stay here to look after you." She declined our request, saying that I took everybody's responsibility on my shoulders and now Dr. Sunandabai had made it to the top of that list. We remained there for about two hours talking about our guru before returning home.

Upon arriving home, I contacted Bhadauriyaji on phone and proposed that from the next day, he and I would stay at Dr. Sunandabai's from 10:00 a.m. to 12 noon, without disturbing her. The following day we reached there at the mutually fixed time. Aunty (I used to call Dr. Sunandabai aunty) took us to her drawing room and showed us her urine report. Everything was normal except for a result suggestive of malaria, but it was not a definite diagnosis. Aunty told me that it was falciparum which was the warning bell of the coming danger. She was reiterating again and again, "Swamiji had told me that I would fall ill only once, and that has already happened. Why am I indisposed again?" (Swamiji's prediction proved true, because she was not to survive this indisposition.) There were some technical details in the report which I failed to understand. Bhadauriyaji immediately rushed to call the physician.

Now only Dr. Sunandabai and I were in the room. She was staring fixedly at the picture of Swamiji without blinking. A stream of tears burst forth from her eyes. She said with folded hands, "I am much indebted to Swamiji. Words fail to describe what he has done and is still doing for me. But I am not in a position to do anything for him." Her tears continued to flow unabated. She made no effort to check them.

In the meantime, Bhadauriyaji returned with a senior doctor. The doctor examined the report and confirmed her fears. We stayed there for some time and then with her permission we left for our respective homes.

After a gap of a day, on Tuesday, the 21st of October both of us again went to see Dr. Sunandabai. That day she was in her personal room. Visitors were usually not allowed there, but she asked me to come in. No sooner did I enter her room than I felt very powerful vibrations pervading the area. As soon as I sat down, I spontaneously started to utter quietly the guru mantra. This was definitely the impact of her regular and sincere prayers and japa performed in that room. She disclosed to me that she had fallen down the previous day and hurt her shoulder, but there was nothing to worry about. I was with her for about two hours. While saying goodbye, I told her that I would be back to stay with her at night and left without waiting for her consent. At about six that evening, Dr. Sunandabai phoned to tell me that she was all right and that there was no need for me to come that night.

The next day, Wednesday, 22nd October, when Bhadauriyaji and I reached her home, we learnt that she had had fever the previous night. In the opinion of the doctors, this was a symptom of the peril ahead. Her health was growing from bad to worse and tending to get out of control, but she was not prepared to accept it. We left her place at about noon, but were anxious about her health all through the day. On Thursday, 23rd October, her neighbor informed me that Dr. Sunandabai's condition was serious. We rushed to her residence, reaching there within five minutes. All her neighbors were already there. She was in her room lying in bed and the ladies were nursing her. Soon, some doctors also arrived. We noticed that her time perception was disturbed. She expressed a desire to eat crisp bread and vegetables and it was fulfilled.

The residence of Dr. Sunandabai was in the vicinity of the Medical College where she had served for many years as the Head of the Department of Gynecology. Therefore, a number of senior doctors who were her students also reached her home upon hearing of her serious condition. They minutely studied her blood report and advised starting an intravenous saline drip. The doctors clearly explained everything to her and wanted her consent. She wanted to know how long it would take. They said that it would start at 2:45 p.m. and continue till 11:45 p.m. Dr. Sunandabai agreed to it. Normal saline was being given intravenously to Dr. Sunandabai. Her students, eminent doctors of the city, were watching her response. They kept a vigil for about an hour and then dispersed, satisfied that things were going well. But after their departure, it was noticed that her hand was swollen at the insertion point of the needle. She herself explained that it was due to lack of blood circulation. At her direction, the infusion was stopped. I was about to go to the adjoining room to inform the doctor, when she said, "What can the doctor do?" Now she was beginning to feel cold and needed a light blanket. By this time, the doctors had come back. As soon as the needle was taken out, she started shivering. Even covered with five blankets, she was shivering. She was continually uttering Hari Om. Getting her instruction, I gave her water by spoon.

Her condition was not improving. One of her students, a senior lady doctor, advised me to shift her to the hospital. She could not muster the courage to seek Dr. Sunandabai's permission herself and asked me to do this for her. After much persuasion, Dr. Sunandabai agreed to be treated in the McRobert

Hospital. Immediately, without losing any time, an ambulance was arranged.

Now, I was left alone with Dr. Sunandabai in her room which was also her place of worship. By this time, her body had become weak Suddenly, she declared, "Gurudeva has arrived. B< w before him with respect and get bedsheets, etc. changed in his room upstairs." Then her voice became indistinct. It appeared as if she were talking with somebody. She was posing questions and the answers were also given in her own voice, but the tone of the questions was low and that of the answers was high. This question-answer sequence made it clear to me that she was conversing with Swamiji. I did not try to hear or follow her further. This conversation lasted for about 30 minutes. In the meantime, I locked the rooms and handed over the keys to Udai Singh. I took her to the ambulance. This conversation continued on the way to the hospital for about 10 minutes.

Dr. Sunandabai was hospitalized at 6:45 p.m. on Thursday. We used to have kirtan every Thursday at our home. After getting Dr. Sunandabai admitted to the hospital, I went home to participate in the kirtan. At the end of the kirtan, I informed the guru disciples present about Dr. Sunandabai's ill health and again rushed to the hospital with my husband Manoj. By 8:30 p.m., I was back in the hospital. Her respiration was not normal but her face was perfectly tranquil. I remained by her side till midnight. I told Bhadauriyaji that I would be back in the morning and left for home.

At 1:15 a.m., Bhadauriyaji gave me a call and in a choked voice asked me to reach the hospital immediately. Without any other indication from him, I inferred that Dr. Sunandabai was no more. I and my husband Manoj rushed to the hospital.

After completing the necessary formalities, we took her body to her residence which she had dedicated to Swamiji and whose ownership she had never claimed. She was cremated that morning, Friday, the 26th of October and the shanti havan was performed the following morning. It was attended by almost all the guru brothers and sisters of Kanpur.

During Dr. Sunandabai's last days, I was with her almost all the time for about six days. During this period, a number of peculiar events occurred. It would not be out of place to mention one of them. On October 22nd she said to me, "Renu, one thought has healed me in every way. Now there is no pain. Previously I used to think that Swami Rama is within everybody; now I realize that everything is Swami Rama." I told her, "Aunty, now what else remains? You have realized your goal." She remarked, "This is what I say. Now what is the use of this physical body?" Hearing her emotional statement, I said, "Please aunty, don't say this, guide us now." She instantly asserted, "No! Find your path in your own way."

My close association with Dr. Sunandabai during this last phase of her life gave me a clear understanding that the guru supports those who fully and completely dedicate themselves to him, in every way, till their last breath. In her last days, none of her relatives were with her. Only we, her guru brothers and sisters, bade her farewell with tearful eyes and chanting of "Gurura Brahma Gurura Vishnu." It would be appropriate to point out that if there is any true relationship in the world, it is that of guru-shishya (teacher-disciple). Dr. Sunandabai was whole heartedly, in mind, speech and action, dedicated to Swamiji. In her life, the guru was all in all, he was supreme.

In the last moments of her worldly voyage, when she was moving from consciousness to unconsciousness, I had a feeling that she was actually advancing in the direction of her identification with consciousness. At this stage, the guru was her support. She had closed her external eyes, but her countenance indicated that she was witness g something wondrous.

The demise of Dr. Sunandabai created a void in my heart for a while, because at every step she was there to clear my spiritual doubts. But the moment I recalled her direction, "Find your path in your own way," I resolved to adhere to that, as far as possible. Then the void disappeared.

I was fortunate to enjoy the company of Dr. Sunandabai from my childhood to adulthood and to observe her lifestyle. She was the embodiment of dedication to the guru. I could know the benefits of devotion through her. Not only this, her closeness revealed to me her reality and her greatness.

She had not registered any will for her movable and immovable properties. She firmly believed that everything belonged to Swamiji. He himself would make proper arrangements. Such devotion for the guru and the integration of mind, speech and action could be seen clearly in the life of Dr. Sunandabai.

While nearing the last phase of her life's journey, signs of changes in her perceptions had become visible. For example, one day when I went to her, she said to me, "Whenever you come here, I have a feeling that Swamiji has arrived." In response to my question, "Why do you say that?" she added, "Because Swami Rama is in you also."

I offer my humble salutations to Dr. Sunandabai.

Blessings from Beyond

By the grace and compassion of Swamiji, the marriage of my elder daughter Arima was fixed to take place in November 2003. In my heart of my hearts, I remembered Swamiji with deep devotion and sought his blessings for the smooth and successful conclusion of this auspicious event.

At that time, prior to the wedding date, my fellow disciple (gurubhai) Ishji came to me one morning and said, "While performing my worship, I felt a strong urge to lend you my recently purchased new car to be used till the celebrations of Arima's marriage are over." With due respect for his feelings, my husband told him that he had already arranged for a number of taxi cabs for the purpose; therefore, there was no need for his car. Next morning, Ishji came again and declared that he was not going to agree to my husband's refusal and delivered the car and its key to him. He was so forceful that we could not decline his offer. We requested him to keep the car at his residence till we had made arrangements for a driver. Only the three of us, Ishji, my husband Manoj and I, knew of this arrangement. It was the day when the auspicious celebration began.

The marriage celebrations concluded in a pleasant atmosphere. The next morning, Arima was given a warm and touching send off and she drove away to the home of her in-laws. In order to observe social tradition, she came back to our home for a short while that same evening, and again returned to her in-laws. After her departure, Manoj suggested that he should get Ishji's car washed and filled with petrol before sending it back to his residence with gratitude. But when Manoj went to instruct the driver, he could not find Ishji's car there. All the other cabs were there. An enquiry about the car was made from the other drivers, but in vain. We tried to find out if any family member had sent the car somewhere. Its whereabouts were unknown to them also.

We were worried about the car. Well wishers advised us to lodge a complaint (FIR: First Information Report) with the police. We did not have the required documents, registration papers, insurance policy, etc. for filing a complaint. We were caught in a dilemma. We decided to contact Ishji to get the required documents. Manoj phoned Ishji and before he could say a word, Ishji said, "You have sent the car back. It is standing here." This information relieved our tension immediately.

The next day, when the driver came for his payment, he was asked why he had returned the car without asking us. His reply was very surprising. "No sooner had Arima been given the send off, than an elderly gentleman from your house came and asked me to return Ishji's car. I obeyed him." When he was asked to give details of the gentleman's appearance, height and attire, he could not tell us very much.

We began to wonder who that elderly gentleman might be. We were perplexed because there was no elderly member in our family. Except for my husband, Ishji and me, no one knew about the car arrangement. On further discussion, we realized that the car had remained with us only so long as the nuptials were being celebrated. Our intuition made us aware of

Swamiji's deep concern for his disciples. It was self-evident.

Another event related to the marriage is worth mentioning. The reception festivities were in progress. The bridegroom's party (barat) had arrived and the pavilion was filled to capacity. In the meantime, I caught sight of the burning upper fringe of the tent. Tents are generally made of a synthetic-mixed yarn. Somebody advised me to put it out immediately but I was unable to do so. At that very moment, I noticed a mechanic rushing there with a ladder. He disconnected the wire and extinguished the fire within the twinkling of an eye. A serious accident was thus averted.

Almost everybody appreciated the arrangements of the marriage, but I was mentally thanking Swamiji. I was thinking that I would be very dishonest if I took the credit for myself. In fact, I was only an instrument in this performance, the performer was someone else.

Our family has been fortunate to live under the canopy of Swamiji's blessings and grace. Swamiji occupies a paramount place in my life. The grace, affection, loving attachment and blessings, which I received from him in abundance since childhood, are my precious treasure. Swamiji did a lot for me but I, a destitute, could not do anything for him. Moreover, he was an unfathomable ocean, while I am only a drop.

Shri K. N. Mehrotra

A Divine Presence

Shri K. N. Mehrotra

Shri K. N. Mehrotra was born in 1937 into a business family of Kanpur, India. He graduated in 1957 with a bachelor's degree in Commerce. He was awarded an M.Com. in 1959 and an L.L.B. in 1961. Initially, he joined the family business. However, later he switched to a career in law and has been practicing civil law in Kanpur for the last 40 years.

In 1959, a friend of his informed him that one Swami Rama was asking for him. However, he had never heard of Swami Rama, till then. He met Swamiji for the first time in April 1959 at Jaipuria House, Kanpur. As soon as Swamiji saw him, he said, "Kailash, I have been with you for the last three lifetimes." This meeting with Swamiji lasted about half an hour and when Kailash emerged, he had become a dedicated follower of Swami Rama. Shri Mehrotra is blessed with a wonderful wife and three sons. Four days after his wedding, Swamiji came to his home to bless him and his young bride. His whole family has enjoyed the guidance and blessings of Swamiji ever since.

My Early Association
with Swami Rama

I met Swami Rama for the first time in the year 1959. He was known as Swami Ram Dandi and conforming to tradition, he carried a Dandi or staff and wore wooden sandals. A few days after my marriage in May 1963, Swami Rama came to Kanpur and wanted to meet my wife. When we went to meet him at the appointed place and hour he was not there. Two hours elapsed, as shown on my wristwatch as well as the wall clock. But amazingly, when he arrived it was the appointed time for our meeting and Swamiji asked everyone to confirm this from the wall clock.

Swamiji visited my home wearing a suit, the coat being slung on his arm. I also wanted him to visit my new house at Ashok Nagar, Kanpur. While traveling in the car of Dr. Gauri Nath Tandon, the renowned Homeopath, Swamiji sketched a drawing of this house. This house was rented out to a tenant. Swamiji advised me to get it vacated and told me how I should go about this. As advised, I got the house vacated the very same day, without having to resort to the law courts.

One night I was sleeping at home and dreamt that Swamiji granted me a vision of the goddess, Mother Durga. In the dream, Swamiji asked me to make an offering to Mother Durga. I protested that I had nothing to offer. He then asked me to make an offering from a bag that he was carrying. I took some money out of the bag and made the offering. Later, that same night, at about 11:30 p.m., Swamiji arrived in person. I tried to tell Swamiji about the dream, but he would not allow me to do so. He asked my mother for something to eat. My mother served him poories and a liquid potato curry. He washed the potatoes in water before eating. When I asked him why, he said that he did not want to eat my salt.

In the year 1955, I got an opportunity to visit Madras accompanied by 10 student friends of mine and two professors. My knowledge of English was very poor, and yet, when we met the Governor of Madras, Shri Sri Prakasam and the Chief Minister, Shri Kamraj Nadar, I spoke in English fluently to my own surprise. Later, in 1959, when Swamiji came into my life, he told me that it was he who had spoken fluent English through me on that visit to Madras.

When Swamiji visited Kanpur, he stayed with Dr. Sunandabai, a renowned gynecologist of Kanpur. I went to visit Swamiji at her home. After parking and locking my bicycle outside the bungalow, I went up to Swamiji's room on the first floor. In the course of the visit, Swamiji suddenly announced that my bicycle had been stolen but that the thief had been caught. He asked me to go and take possession of the bicycle.

One day, I went to meet Swamiji around 9:00 p.m. Swamiji had to go somewhere and asked me to wait for him outside the bungalow on the road. I just kept on waiting. When he returned, he asked me if I knew what time it was. It was 3:00 a.m. He asked me why I was still there. When I reminded him that he had asked me to wait, he smiled. I did not have any personal transport at that time. Somehow, Swamiji arranged for me to reach my residence in the cheapest and quickest possible way. I really do not know how he managed that!

Swami Rama
My Mysterious Master

I had a burning desire to know what Swamiji
did during the night. He allowed me to accompany
him one night. We went to the bank of the Ganges
at Kanpur which was in full flood. I saw an animal
floating in the flood waters. Swamiji asked me, "Do
you know what that is?" I answered that it was a cat.
But Swamiji said, "No, it is the soul of a disciple who
has come to seek my permission to depart from this
world." The next day, the mother of Dr. Gauri Nath
Tandon, a disciple of Swamiji passed away. Swamiji
was present at her cremation.

When this lady was on her deathbed at Birhana
Road, Kanpur, Swamiji had instructed the family that
the Ramayan be read daily for at least four hours in
the evening. I happened to be doing the daily reading
one day when Swamiji dropped in. Swamiji instructed
me to read the Ramayan in a particular manner. Later,
when I heard the tape of Ramayan by Swamiji, I
understood what he had taught me.

Even after building a new house for myself, I
continued to live in the old house. There was a picture
of Swamiji in the new house. One of my cousins, who
had a lot of animosity towards my father and was
plotting to oust my father from the family business,
was once visiting the new house. At the same time,
around 9:30 p.m., Swamiji asked me to meet him at
Birhana Road, Kanpur where he was staying for a

short while. When I went there, Swamiji enabled me to hear, word for word, as if I were listening to a tape recorder, the entire planning and plotting that my cousin was indulging in, five miles away! The sounds stopped when the plotting stopped. On the day of the birth of my eldest son (July 19th ,1968), Swamiji signed as a witness the papers ending the family partnership and advised me to take charge of the Lucknow shop where he arranged for a ritual puja and changed the name of the firm.

My younger brother was engaged to be married and during the celebration, he was forced to consume an overdose of bhang by my cousin's son. My brother was totally imbalanced by the drug overdose and started behaving in an irrational manner. As a consequence, his marriage engagement was broken off. My brother went to consult Swamiji with his tutor, Mr. Dixit and my cousin's son. Swamiji was then at Agra. When my brother reached Agra, Swamiji offered him his own bed and instructed him to lock the door from inside. He was asked to open the door after one hour. He failed to do so, explaining that he was enjoying himself very much there and had never before experienced such happiness. Swamiji ordered him to open the door or else he would break through the closed door. Finally, my brother did open the door. When he came out, he was completely sound in body and mind. All the madness was gone.

We went to Dr. Gauri Nath Tandon's house in Kanpur to finalize the details of this brother's marriage that Swamiji had arranged. While this meeting was going on, Swamiji suddenly asked all of us to leave the room and he locked it from the inside. Later, when he opened the door and came out, he told us that he was speaking with the departed soul of Pandit Jawaharlal Nehru, the Prime Minister of India. We switched on the radio at his request and heard for ourselves the announcement of Pandit Jawaharlal Nehru's death.

There was a conference organized by the Medical College of Jhansi which I attended. Two yoga instructors, Mr. Kulkarni and Mr. Mahesh Dwivedi, also attended the conference and we were received by the Principal of the college himself. Mr. Dwivedi was, like me, a student of the first batch of yoga classes started by Swamiji at Kanpur. At the conference, Swamiji showed how, by the power of yoga, he could control his circulation, displaying two different colors on the ankle of his right foot.

I once attended a conference in Delhi inaugurated by Vasant Sathe, the Union Minister. I stayed in the railway retiring room with Mr. Gopi Kishan Khare, a leading criminal lawyer of Kanpur and Mr. Prabhakar Tewari, a retired person from the military who later was the Deputy Labor Commissioner at Kanpur. I carried with me a sealed envelope addressed to Swamiji sent by Mr. Kulkarni. Without even opening the envelope, Swamiji told me, "I am always with the person who has given you this envelope, but he does not realize this." He returned the envelope to me. That same evening, he wanted me to go to the residence of a doctor who had had steel braces on his body. The doctor had met Swamiji in the U.S. and Swamiji had cured him to the extent that the steel braces had been removed. When I reached the doctor's residence, Swamiji saw me but left without speaking to me. When I went inside, Dr. Usharbudh Arya (now Swami Veda Bharatiji) was there. He also mentioned the sealed envelope and started telling me what was written inside without even opening it. The letter had been written by Mr. Kulkarni, who was running the yoga classes of the Manohar Lal Dudeja Trust that Swamiji had inaugurated in the year 1972. When I returned and narrated the incident to Mr. Kulkarni he was very surprised.

I had been wanting to offer fruits to Swamiji on the sacred day of Guru Purnima but unfortunately, I could not, as Swamiji was usually overseas at that time of the year. I decided to offer all the fruits into a well in Lucknow. Upon his return, Swamiji said to me, "I did eat the fruits you sent me through the well."

Swamiji's Solicitious Concern for Our Family

Once at Lucknow, the father of Ashok Tandon phoned me, asking me to meet Swamiji who was passing through Lucknow on his way to Sitapur. It was about 5:00 p.m., and I had just reached the given place when a Fiat car stopped by my side. I saw Swamiji sitting quietly in it, accompanied by Dr. Mittra, a renowned Homeopath living in Arya Nagar, Kanpur. Dr. Mittra indicated that I should occupy the front seat beside the driver. Swamiji was observing silence. We then started going towards Sitapur. About 45 minutes later, I began to think about my return to Lucknow. At the same time, Swamiji instructed the driver to change the direction towards Lucknow to the residence of Dr. Khanna, where about 30 people were waiting to welcome Swamiji. Swamiji, in his lecture, spoke about the benefits of hatha yoga. I understood that Swamiji was in silence during the journey as he was preparing to address the Lucknow gathering. At the end of his lecture, he told me that my first son was having a skin problem on his scalp. He had brought Dr. Mittra along to treat my son. He instructed Dr. Mittra to check my son, who was then sent back to Kanpur for treatment. This incident made me realize how solicitously Swamiji was looking after my family.

My son Rupesh was four months old when I took him with me to receive Swamiji at the Kanpur airport. Swamiji took Rupesh in his lap and declared that the child was his and I was only the custodian. He made me promise that I would allow Swamiji to claim him back and announced this to the others there. Years later, Rupesh appeared for an engineering final exam. Before the results could be declared, I took him with me to Jolly Grant to visit Swamiji. Swamiji reminded me of my promise and ordered me to leave Rupesh behind when I returned to Kanpur, as he was now claiming what was his. Rupesh is in Jolly Grant to this day.

I once went to meet Swamiji at Sitapur. Swamiji gave me some instructions. It was late in the night and my wife had accompanied me. There was no conveyance to be had for miles around at that time of the night. Suddenly, one of his disciples arrived on a motor bike. Swamiji arranged for the disciple to take us home, my wife and I, both riding pillion on the bike.

Once, Swamiji wanted to visit my in-laws at Kaushalpuri, Kanpur. There was not a single car out of three family cars available at that time, so he came along with me in a cycle rickshaw. On the way back, he advised me to arrange the delivery of my first child at the clinic of Dr. Lashmi Sehgal, a renowned gynecologist who had been associated with the famous patriot Netaji Subhash Chandra Bose. He also asked me what career I wanted to pursue. When I told him that I wanted to serve the public by becoming a bus conductor, he said, "No! I will decide."

Once, Swamiji asked me to come to Mr. Kotiwal's residence in Swaroop Nagar, Kanpur. It was late evening and Swamiji was playing the sitar, accompanied on the tabla by Pandit Laxmi Narain Tiwari, a disciple of Swamiji. I was really surprised to see Swamiji's masterly command of the sitar.

On a visit to Allahabad to meet Swamiji, my younger brother told me that Swamiji had dictated to him a book that was soon to be reléased, titled, *Yug Dharma Kya Hai?* I read it on the flight from Kathmandu to Patna and wrote a review of the book which I showed Swamiji. Swamiji wanted me to have it published in the local Hindi newsp　 ᴐer of Kanpur named *Vartman*. He told me that they ᵥould publish the review only if the title Pandit preceded my name. Swamiji made me add the title Pandit to my name. The review was published and I presented a copy of the publication to Swamiji.

Once on a visit to Bahraich for business, I was walking to the railway station late one night, around 11:30 p.m. I saw a stick on the right side of the road. Only after picking it up did I realize that it was a snake. All I know is that I said sorry to the snake and it went away without harming me. When I met Swamiji, he suddenly remarked that if you do not harm any creature, it will never harm you under any circumstances, and that the word sorry was understood even by those who did not know the language; what mattered was the feeling, not the words.

One day Swamiji came to the yoga center at 7:30 p.m. and asked me to wait. It was the day before the festival of Diwali. A box of mithai (sweets) was brought for Swamiji and left with my friend, the yoga instructor, Mr. Gopi Chand Arora. Mr. Arora claimed that he was very hungry and wanted to open the box of mithai and have some sweets. He tried to persuade me to join in, saying that Swamiji would want us to have some too. I firmly refused. He just would not stop pressuring me to take some sweets. To avoid his pressure, I ran and hid in the bathroom till Swamiji returned. Swamiji asked about me and when the episode was narrated, he appreciated my behavior.

Experiences with Swamiji in Rishikesh and at Jolly Grant

Once Swamiji called me to Rishikesh, where he was living in Kali Kambli Walla Ashram adjoining Sadhana Mandir Ashram, which was not in existence at that time. He asked me how much money I had in my pocket. When I told him, he gave me some more money and the electric bill, asking me to pay it. I then had to write to the father of Ashok Tandon in Kanpur, (elder brother of Dr. Gauri Nath Tandon) to send a money order for Rs. 300 in my name. Swamiji accepted the money order. He gave me this money and some more, asking me to pay the house tax and water tax bills. This way, he taught me how to travel without money. I have since adopted this trait; if I have money it is good; if I do not, I still manage to get all the comforts that even a lot of money cannot buy.

As Swamiji used to smoke, I started sending cigarette packets to his ashram at Rishikesh. On meeting him, I asked him why he smoked. He said that he smoked to chase people away so that he could remain in solitude.

A very destructive earthquake hit the state of Uttarakhand in 1991. Swamiji played a major role in the relief effort and adopted some of the affected villages. I was curious to see what kind of help was required and how Swamiji was providing relief. Swamiji allowed me to tour the villages and I traveled in the medical van of a Kanpur hospital with the slogan

"Eyes on Wheels." A wash basin was attached inside the back of the van. An apprehensive doctor asked me if I had ever traveled in the mountains and wisely gave me a tablet for travel sickness. Initially, I did not wish to take the tablet, but changed y mind at the first stop. I was vomiting all the way to the adopted village. Swamiji was following us in his car. When we reached the village, Swamiji announced at the public meeting that "one of my disciples came here vomiting all the way."

Later during the meeting, Swamiji happened to be drowsing with his mouth slightly open. I looked into his mouth and an amazing sight met my eyes. I saw the movement of the Kala Chakra, the Wheel of Time, bodies being born, bodies experiencing the joys and sorrows of life, and bodies being consumed by death. It was like the vision of a multitude of galaxies and universes that Yashoda, the mother of Lord Krishna witnessed, when she forced his mouth open upon suspecting that he had been eating mud.

After the public meeting, Swamiji asked me to stay overnight at the Government (PWD) Guest House where he had arranged for a very comfortable stay. He wanted me to tour the villages the next day to find out if the financial assistance that he was providing the villagers was being properly utilized. The help he had provided was to be distributed based on the number of family members, their status and income before the earthquake and their needs. Some goons of the area were trying to prevent the villagers from accepting the financial help that was being provided. It was done so systematically and cleverly that it was beyond my imagination. These bad elements were forcibly trying to take away the help being provided. When I met Swamiji again, he remarked that he had wanted me to stay the night there in order to see for myself how the villagers were being harassed.

When the Himalayan Hospital was almost ready, I was invited by Swamiji to his apartment on the campus. It was raining very heavily and the drain pipes and drains were flooded with the rain waters. The campus was looking very attractive. Swamiji remarked, "It's like heaven on earth."

When the date for the inauguration of the Himalayan Hospital had been fixed, I sought Swamiji's permission to attend the ceremony. He said, "No!" When I met Swamiji after the inauguration, he asked me why I was not at the ceremony.

Swamiji wanted me to come to his ashram in Rishikesh for the celebration of the festival of Shivratri. When I reached at 4:30 a.m., Swamiji's watch dogs began to bark ferociously. However, the caretaker took charge and directed me to a room to rest. I was asked to be ready by 7:30 a.m., to escort a group of foreign guests to the Himalayan Hospital as directed by Swamiji. I willingly lead the group on foot to the bus stand and we travelled to the hospital by bus. The bus conductor dropped us off at a stop which was not very close to the hospital; so once again we had to walk. Unfortunately, when we arrived, a complaint had already been made against me to Swamiji for subjecting the group to so much walking. But Swamiji explained to them that it was not my fault that the group had been dropped off so far from the hospital. Swamiji's defense of my actions diffused the resentment, and members of the group have now become my pen friends!

Once, I was on an evening walk with Swamiji and another disciple at Jolly Grant. Swamiji asked us both a legal question. My answer, however, differed from that of the other disciple. Swamiji was pleased with my answer and said it was correct, whereas, the other disciple's answer was politically motivated, as he was closely connected with some top leaders in Delhi.

According to me, those who thought of Swamiji as an ordinary human being, experienced immense grief when he departed the body, whereas, those who looked upon him as divine are still getting instructions from him. I experience the presence of Swamiji every now and then, in my sleeping hours in dreams, and in my meditation, irrespective of time and place. Sometimes even when I am not sleepy, he creates sleep in me in order to give me a particular instruction. Thus he taught me, and continues to teach me in various ways.

Hema de Munnik
୬

A Life Transformed

Hema

Hema (Hendrika Louise de Munnik) was born in 1937 in Amsterdam, the Netherlands. She served as a child psychologist and lecturer in psychology till 1990. In 1991 she met her spiritual teacher, Swami Rama in Curacao, where she taught hatha yoga at the Himalayan Institute of Curacao. In 1995 she moved to Swami Rama's ashram in Rishikesh, India. From 1997 till 2006 she was engaged in selfless service at the Himalayan Hospital founded by Swami Rama in Dehradun. In 2005, Hema authored a book titled *Bhole: Adventures of a Young Yogi, inspired by the childhood stories of Swami Rama.* In 2006, Hema returned to the Netherlands, living in Putten, during the summer and in Villajoyoa, Spain in the winter. She is the mother of Judea and Martin and the grandmother of Luma and Ella.

Transformation: Phase 1

In the spring of 1991, I learnt from a local newspaper in Curacao, about a weekend seminar on yoga, "Ancient and Modern Therapies," organized by the Himalayan Institute.

That weekend became a major turning point in my life. The timing was perfect. I had just left my Antillean partner and my dreams of happily growing old with this wonderful man had been shattered to pieces. I was still very much in love with him, and deeply disappointed that our relationship hadn't worked out.

I moved into a small studio where I tried to keep myself busy with my latest interest: holistic health exercises (called joints and glands at the Himalayan Institute) and hatha yoga postures. Six months earlier, a friend had introduced me to a nearby yoga school to work on my menopause and stress-related problems. I loved the calm and peaceful atmosphere of the place and the exercises did me good.

There was a small shop attached to it, where I found a book by Paramahansa Yogananda, *Autobiography of a Yogi*. I bought it, started reading, and couldn't stop till I had finished it. I was elated because this book gave answers to questions that I had pondered since childhood. This book, and the effect of the yoga exercises, gave me the strength to choose for myself and to finish the painful relationship with my partner.

When I read in the newspaper that a certain Swami Rama was one of the speakers at the seminar, I asked my yoga teacher what kind of a man this swami was. He said that Swami Rama was a good psychologist and a kind of no-nonsense swami. I decided to attend the seminar, mainly because I didn't want to be alone over the weekend. I had no idea that this decision would change my life completely.

The lectures by Phil Nuernberger, Dr. Clarke, Shanta, Aruna Bhargava and Pandit Rajmani Tigunait fell like seeds on fertile soil. I wrote down almost every word they said, because everything seemed important to me. Here I was finally getting clear guidelines on how to meditate.

Since the early 1980s, when I spent a summer in the U.S., I had been puzzled by this phenomenon called meditation. Many of my Californian friends were meditators but none of them could give me clear information about what they were doing and what actually happened during these sessions.

A few years later, I attended a seminar "Exploring our Deep Ecology" at the Findhorn Foundation in Scotland, where we did awareness exercises outdoors. At a certain moment the group decided to sit down to meditate. I also sat down and closed my eyes but didn't know what else to do. The rock on which I sat was hard and uncomfortable and my back was aching. I really don't know what happened next, but when I opened my eyes, the group had already left and I was still sitting on that hard rock, experiencing a kind of lightness and happiness that I had never known before. Had I been meditating? I didn't know, but it felt so good that I wanted more of it. During my week in Findhorn I experienced this wonderful sensation once more when I walked all by myself in the woods.

When the yoga school in Curacao announced a group meditation, I decided to attend. That evening I felt very much out of place, sitting with my back against a wall, not knowing what to do and how to start. The people around me were doing something I wasn't able to, and I felt frustrated that the wonderful Findhorn experience didn't come back.

I joined a meditation group in Curacao, hoping to learn meditation. I participated in a course, given by one of its members, but even that didn't give me much clarity about the subject. I began to consider myself a person unfit for meditation.

During the seminar by the Himalayan Institute, I was taught how to sit and how to relax and breathe properly and how to deal with the thoughts that were always present in my mind. I also learnt to use the soham mantra with the breath. Somehow I felt that this was very important.

Swami Rama and his lecture on the Bhagavad Gita didn't impress me very much. Since my childhood I had doubts about so-called holy men. To me, Swami Rama looked like a combination of my former father-in-law, whom I didn't like very much, and Sinterklaas, a fake saint, in the attire of a bishop, who gives presents to the children in Holland on the fifth of December (a kind of Dutch Father Christmas).

I must have been four years old, when on the evening of the fifth of December, Sinterklaas visited my home in Amsterdam and gave me a doll's house. I remember two things that didn't seem quite right that evening. The first was that Sinterklaas was wearing my father's shoes. The second was that earlier, I had found the doll's house hidden behind a closet and had secretly played with it while my parents were at work.

That Sinterklaas evening I felt very lonely because I realized that the adults in the family were lying to me. This was the first time in my life I doubted the reliability of adults, including my parents, who wanted me to believe that Sinterklaas had come all the way from Spain to bring me a doll's house. Later experiences in my life confirmed my doubts and taught me never to trust adults and so-called authorities.

I remember that when Swami Rama appeared on the stage, he immediately reminded me of my father dressed like Sinterklaas (I even wanted to peek to find out if he was wearing my father's shoes). His English was hard to understand and it took me a while to make something of it.

When he began to talk about his childhood and said that he had never been attached to his parents, I became interested. As a child psychologist I had worked with children with attachment problems, and here I expected to meet an interesting case. I even wondered if the way he dressed had something to do with not having had a mother telling him: "Hey boy, get dressed!" when he was still wearing his morning gown at lunchtime.

The rest of his lecture, as far as I could understand, confused me because I disagreed with almost everything he said. He talked about a book, the Bhagavad Gita, which I didn't know. He spoke about a certain Arjuna, who didn't want to fight and kill. For me, a survivor of the German occupation during the Second World War and one who had been active in the peace movement in Holland in the eighties, non-fighting and non-killing were the most important things in my life. I thought that yoga agreed with this philosophy, but here was this swami from India saying that Arjuna should fight and kill, not only his enemies, but even his relatives and teachers. This was not something I wanted to hear and I didn't really pay attention to the rest of his lecture.

I decided that although I liked the people of the Himalayan Institute, the swami was not someone I wanted to meet. He was too different from everything I stood for. That evening after the cultural program, we were invited for kirtan under the stars with Swami Rama. I went home because I wasn't interested in the swami and also didn't know what kirtan was.

At home I read and reread my notes and started practicing according to the guidelines given. I decided that this was going to be my way to learn meditation, and made a firm resolve to continue practicing until it worked. I made myself a meditation seat and improvised a mosquito net, because the sanguras (small, almost invisible mosquitoes) of Curacao do not respect aspirant meditators.

Between my papers, I found a leaflet I had picked up from a table at the seminar. It was about a guided tour to India in the fall. I had never before considered visiting India, but in my depressed state of mind I needed something to look forward to; so I decided to sign up.

In the months that followed, interesting things happened. I kept attending the yoga classes and my physical flexibility and ability to concentrate improved a lot. That helped me with my sitting posture and soon I was able to sit straight for some time without my back hurting. But the real meditation experience hadn't come yet.

Instead of feeling happiness and bliss, it often happened that I cried or that strong emotions like anger and anxiety popped up, unexpectedly. I had always considered myself a peaceful person, but seated on my meditation cushion, I discovered a fair amount of aggression coming from within. Once I even saw myself sitting in the back of a pickup truck, shooting with a machine gun at my former partner's house!

In the past, these things would have upset me, but from the lectures at the seminar and from Swami Rama's books I learnt to let them go, to stop giving them attention and to go back to the mantra. That worked, but I was still impatiently waiting for the real meditation to happen.

One morning I was so discouraged that I prayed to the Lord, "Please, at least once give me a sign that shows that I'm on the right track with this practice." And lo and behold something happened at once! Instead of thoughts circling around in my head, I saw something, a crystal clear image that I could never have conjured up myself. It appeared before my mind's eye and even now, more than 20 years later, I can see the details. It puzzled me and I didn't understand its meaning, but it was at least the kind of unusual experience that, according to me, could have something to do with real meditation.

One evening, in the middle of my meditation practice, I suddenly felt that I should open my eyes. Just in time, because a big fat lisinbein (a centipede), the largest I have ever seen, came crawling straight towards me. Its bite can be as dangerous as that of a scorpion; so I thanked the Lord for having warned me. Now I knew that l was not alone when I tried to meditate.

That summer I met new people and made new friends in the meditation group. Together we studied the books of Rudolf Steiner, the founder of Anthroposophy. I had been interested in these books during my adolescent years but forgot them after I got married. Now it felt good to read and discuss Steiner's thoughts with other people; but my main interest was still yoga.

My daughter Judea also lived in Curacao, where she tried to make a living as a painter of landscapes and portraits. One day she was asked to paint a life-size portrait of somebody's guru for his meditation room. She needed the money badly, so she accepted a payment in advance to buy canvas and oil paint. The disciple gave her a photograph of Sathya Sai Baba and wanted the work ready before his birthday, a few weeks later.

Usually my daughter works fast, but this time she tried and tried but wasn't content with the result. The face of this Sai Baba was very hard to paint. The day the portrait had to be ready was almost upon her, and she was very unhappy about the situation, because she had already spent the money. A friend, who knew something about Sathya Sai Baba, told us that he was an Indian saint who could do miracles. Of course we didn't believe that, and laughed about it. He also said that she could ask Sai Baba for help if she needed it. That sounded even more ridiculous! But what does one do when the portrait has to be ready within a week? My daughter still finds it hard to admit that she took my friend's advice and asked Sai Baba to help her. After that the work was successfully completed within a few days.

When the disciple came to pick up the large painting, he was happy with it. I happened to be there at the time and asked him if he could tell me something about this Sai Baba. He said that I had better read books about him and the next day he delivered a pile of books at my house. My daughter and I read all of them and we were very surprised to learn about a world where things that we couldn't believe to be true, happened.

I was still very skeptical about these stories and decided that to be able to really believe the miraculous things Sai Baba was supposed to perform, I had to see them with my own eyes; so I decided to extend my trip to India by a few months in order to visit Sai Baba's ashram in Puttaparthi. I also hoped to meet a few other interesting gurus in India. I had this romantic picture in my mind of Paramahamsa Yogananda finding his guru Sri Yukteswar in a small alley somewhere in an old Indian town. That was my dream too and in this way the excursion, organized by the Himalayan Institute, became a big adventure.

Before I left Curacao that summer, friends gave me letters to be delivered to Sai Baba and my daughter also decided to write one. She included a picture of her painting and asked Sai Baba if he could fulfill her dearest wish of many years — a child. She said, "If he really is God, he must be able to fulfill my wish."

To escape the summer heat in Curacao, I went to Amsterdam, visited my son and his Japanese girlfriend, and stayed in the apartment of a friend, who was on vacation in India. I tried to continue my hatha and meditation practice and prepared myself for the trip by reading books about the culture of India. In the apartment, I found a handout about eastern philosophy and yoga, as taught at the Philosophy Department of the University of Amsterdam. It said exactly what I believed before I read Paramahamsa Yogananda's book: "The claims of yoga and meditation are unscientific, un-Christian and dangerous, because practicing yoga and meditation can have negative consequences for one's mental health." Since my experiences with yoga were exactly the opposite, I now strongly disagreed.

The third week of September I flew from Amsterdam to New Delhi, where I was to join the group from the U.S. I was nervous because this part of the world was absolutely unknown to me. I expected to become overwhelmed by filth, chaos and difficulties and was surprised to meet exactly the opposite. The airport bus dropped me at the Hyatt Regency Hotel. Never in my life had I been in such a beautiful and luxurious place. The group from the U.S. hadn't arrived yet and I had a whole day to look around and to bathe in luxury.

In the afternoon my friends from Amsterdam came to see me. They showed me a little of New Delhi and then took me by auto rickshaw to Old Delhi, where they wanted to visit a famous mosque. The narrow streets were very crowded and as the rickshaw driver couldn't take us further, we had to walk. This was the first time in my life that I was walking in the streets of Old Delhi; the strange thing was that I felt perfectly at ease. The crowd, the noises, the smells, the cows and other animals, they all belonged there; I felt I did too. I even thought I knew the way through the narrow alleys to the mosque and got the strong feeling that I had been there before. That deep feeling of being home never left me during the years I lived in India.

The next day, the Himalayan Institute group arrived and the first person I met was Yona, a young woman who told me that she also wanted to stay longer than the three weeks of the excursion. We immediately agreed to travel together to South India.

With the group we went to Agra to visit the Taj Mahal. I was glad to be part of a group of foreigners, because had I been alone, the culture shock would have been too much for me. Having traveled in Morocco and Curacao, I thought I was more or less culture shock proof, but in India everything was so different from what I was used to, I would have felt completely lost, had I been there all by myself.

Next door to the Hyatt hotel a new building was under construction. I was shocked when I saw that all day long, fragile women had to carry heavy baskets with cement and stones on their heads, while the men were guiding heavily loaded donkeys, or were just sitting there, doing nothing at all.

On the way to the early morning train to Agra, we had to step over people, even families with babies and young children, who were sleeping on the dirty platform. When the train took off, I noticed a row of people squatting to defecate along the railway tracks next to the train.

In the evening, we were invited by an Indian family to their beautiful house where we were offered a delicious meal. Children in traditional costumes danced for us. This was my first visit to an Indian home and I was deeply impressed. It was a spacious and modern house, with a guard in front of the entrance. In the new, American style kitchen, I noticed a statue of a lady in a white sari, sitting cross legged on top of the kitchen counter, where in Holland we usually put the coffee maker. I also peeked into the puja room, where the family worshipped their gods, and wondered why they also kept their bicycles there.

A tourist bus took us to Rishikesh, where we stayed in Swami Rama's Ashram. I immediately fell in love with the place and with the Ganga river. It felt so good to sit on the steps leading to the water and to watch the hazy blue mountains and the gently flowing silvery green stream. At dawn, the voices of women chanting prayers were coming over the water. I could easily understand that in India people consider this river to be a goddess. Heaven couldn't be more beautiful than this.

In the ashram I stayed in a dorm with seven other women and there was a lot of talking, which I didn't like very much. I needed quiet to let the new impressions sink in and always looked for a place where I could be alone to read or write.

I also didn't like the way some of the women were responding to the presence of Swami Rama. Around their mattresses they had put several of his pictures and they talked about him the way teenagers talk about their favorite pop star. When he walked in the garden, they ran after him, just to look at him or to attract his attention. I didn't understand this behavior at all.

Being born in Amsterdam in 1937, a time when many people in Germany, and in Holland too, adored Adolf Hitler, I remember my mother telling me never to put a human being on a pedestal, because that had been the cause of World War II. So instead of going outside to look at the swami, I stayed in a quiet corner behind the meditation hall, or sat near the Ganga.

One afternoon, when I walked with one of my American dormmates in the direction of the dining room, we saw Swami Rama coming towards us. I don't know exactly how it happened, but suddenly the lady was lying flat on the footpath with her face at his feet. I first thought that she had tripped over something and wanted to help her up, but Swami Rama kicked her softly with his foot and said, in a not very friendly tone, "Stop that nonsense, do your practice!" I felt sorry for the lady who had this accident in front of her guru and didn't understand Swami Rama's reaction. To me he seemed very arrogant and unkind, and once more I thought that I didn't want to get to know this man.

We made an excursion into the Himalayan mountains, and visited the area where Swami Rama was born. Dr. Awashti, an Indian teacher who spoke English, was appointed to help us and we could ask him anything. I had lots of questions because I didn't understand much of Indian culture and religion and he patiently answered all of them. I remember that, when we visited a town called Landsdown, we saw a military training camp and in the temple was a big statue of the goddess Durga. At that time I wondered why the Indians had chosen a female to guide them in times of war instead of a male. I think I was one of the most ignorant foreigners who ever visited India, but I was one hundred percent curious and wanted to find out and learn about everything.

Back in the ashram, I wrote long letters to my family and friends in Holland and Curacao. I felt that I was in the middle of a process of transformation and feared that they wouldn't recognize and accept me anymore. At that time I didn't know that the biggest change was yet to come.

I enjoyed the stay in the ashram very much. Every afternoon there were wonderful hatha classes, where I learned many new things. I also learned more about relaxation and my body and mind absorbed it with great joy. In the evening we sat under a big tent and Swami Rama would sing with us. I've always been a lover of music and played the piano since my sixth year, but this Indian music was a real challenge.

In the beginning I had great difficulty listening to it and didn't understand it at all. When Swami Rama began to sing, I thought: "Ah, this man shouldn't sing anymore. He is too old. There is a terrible tremor in his voice and he is out of tune most of the time." To my surprise everybody around me considered him a wonderful singer. To my ears every note he sang was horribly false. When he announced a concert by a famous Indian lady singer, I was looking forward to some really good singing, but was flabbergasted when she produced even more strange and out of tune sounds than Swami Rama did. Apparently I needed to learn more about Indian music to be able to appreciate it. That's why I decided to look for an Indian music teacher in Curacao, to learn to understand and appreciate Indian classical music.

In the last week of our stay we could ask for a personal interview with Swami Rama. Everybody immediately wrote his or her name on a list that had been put up in the library. Although there had been moments when I considered asking him for another mantra than soham, I wasn't interested in becoming his devotee and didn't sign up. When I noticed that I was the only one who didn't want to meet the swami, I thought it a bit impolite, if I didn't use this opportunity to thank him for the wonderful time in his ashram. I thought, "I will just say thank you and that will be it."

A few minutes before the list was taken away, I added my name. I was a bit nervous because I had heard that Swami Rama could read people's minds and I didn't want him to find out what I really thought of him.

The next morning, people gathered in the library, waiting to be seen by Swami Rama. I was told that the list was too long for one morning; I should come back in the afternoon, but stay in the area, in case he called me earlier. This waiting really spoiled my precious day and I regretted very much that I had signed up. The whole afternoon I spent sitting in the dark library, and at the end I was told to come back the next morning because Swamiji was tired. I was very irritated by this seeing-the-swami-thing.

The next morning my turn came and Ragani showed me into the room where Swami Rama was reclining on a few big cushions. I was nervous and shy and didn't have much to say. He was very friendly and asked me where I was from. When he heard that

I lived in Curacao and was interested in yoga and meditation, he immediately said, "I will make you a yoga teacher." I weakly protested and said, "But I'm already over 50." He didn't listen and asked, "Do you want to establish a Himalayan Institute in Curacao?" I didn't know what to answer because I wasn't sure if he was serious or not. I didn't consider myself fit for establishing anything in Curacao. I was but a guest on the island, and as a Dutch person (a makamba), not very much appreciated by the local people. Curacao has been a colony of the Netherlands since 1815, and in 1991, still had a semi-independent status.

Then he said, "Come back Thursday morning at six o'clock; first take a bath, wash your hair, put on clean clothes and then come to me and I'll give you a mantra." Before I knew it I was outside, thinking, "What is happening to me? How can I ever become a yoga teacher? How can I establish a Himalayan Institute? I don't even know what a Himalayan Institute is!"

Then serious doubts entered my mind. "Do I really want this mantra? What kind of effect will it have on me? Will I become like the ladies in the dorm, participating in a personality cult? Do I want to be a yoga teacher in Curacao, establishing a Himalayan Institute?" Gone was my peace of mind.

When I told a few people what Swami Rama had said, they congratulated me. Being initiated by Swami Rama himself seemed to be a big deal. How could I possibly deny this offer? I felt kind of trapped and needed to make up my mind, so I sat down on the steps of the Ganga and prayed to the Lord to help me with this dilemma. After some time it was as if my doubts and anxieties were washed away by the stream of silvery water and were replaced by feelings of joy and gratitude.

The day before the initiation, every so often, the doubts came back, but I was calm and decided to let things happen and see what would come of it. If this mantra would help me to become a better meditator, it was worth trying.

I'll never forget that Thursday. It was the 3rd of October 1991. I got up when it was still dark, took a shower in the sparsely illuminated and icy-cold bathroom, and washed my hair with almost cold water; very unpleasant for a person used to a life of luxury on a tropical island. I waited in the library until I was called upstairs and was very nervous.

Swami Rama didn't seem well that day. Unkempt and unshaven, he reclined on his cushions, coughing badly and spitting into a spittoon. Next to him was a tray with incense, some water, red powder and a small red rose. I had brought a walkman and he placed it between us on the floor. He made sure that it worked and then told me the mantra. The Sanskrit words didn't mean anything to me. He wrote the words on a piece of paper and made a drawing of the symbol that I had to visualize and concentrate on. He made me repeat the words a few times until my pronunciation was correct.

Then he explained the meaning of the words, while putting some red powder on my forehead and in my hair, crushing the rose in his hand and putting its petals on my head and in my two palms. All of this caused an incredible sensation! When he touched my forehead it was as if a wave of electricity ran along my spine. It gave me goose bumps and I felt my hairs stand on end. For a few moments I was completely gone, like when I was at Findhorn.

What struck me too was the meaning of the mantra and I wondered, "How does he know this? How did he find out that this thought has been my solace in good and bad times since my earliest childhood? I've always lived with these words, not knowing that they were a mantra. If he knows me that well, he must be my God-given guru."

Then he looked at me with incredible love in his eyes that went straight to my heart and said with a soft and kind voice, "From now on I am your spiritual father. You are my child and I'll take care of all your needs," and with a twinkle, "but not of all your wants."

The word father touched me deeply and brought tears into my eyes. I haven't had a father since my sixth year and now suddenly I had one. This was too good to be true. At that moment, Swami Rama had another coughing spell and immediately the image of my coughing and blood-spitting father came into my mind and I thought, "You are my father now, but don't you dare die of lung cancer like my first father did!"

Swamiji said,"Remember your mantra always, and it will bring you where you want to be. Come to Honesdale in the U.S. for further training and keep practicing."

I really needed time for myself after this, but an excursion was scheduled to the leper colony in Dehradun and to the hospital under construction which I didn't want to miss. So I was physically present, but my mind was somewhere else, digesting what had happened. I tried to remember the Sanskrit words of the mantra as often as possible and then, bit by bit, the real impact of the initiation became clear to me. It felt as if a huge plough had turned over the soil of my heart, to make new growth possible.

A few days later, the group went back to Delhi, staying again in the beautiful Hyatt hotel. We were invited to an Indian wedding that night and some American ladies told me how wonderful and inexpensive the beauty parlor in the hotel was. I was suffering from a cold and didn't feel well and they said that a facial massage would do me good. I had never before visited a beauty parlor and decided to join them and to ask the people there to help me put on the sari that I had bought in Rishikesh, especially for the wedding.

The ladies of the beauty parlor must have thought that they did a wonderful job, putting makeup on my face and dressing me like a Barbie doll. When I came back to my room and looked in the mirror, I was horrified. I really didn't recognize myself. I looked like something between a witch and a caricature of a mother-in-law in a cheap theatre play; the group was already leaving, so there wasn't time to change. When I walked into the lobby, I saw in the eyes of the other ladies, how terrible I looked and the whole evening I tried to stay in the dark.

The wedding though was interesting, completely different from what we are used to in the West. I took lots of photographs to show to the people at home. We were offered very nice food, but I ate very little because I was suffering from a cold and from indigestion since we left the ashram.

Before the group left for the U.S. the next evening, we were invited to a room in the hotel to say goodbye to Swami Rama. Yona and I arranged to stay a few more days in the Hyatt to prepare for the rest of our trip. When Swami Rama asked me what my plans were, I answered that I wanted to stay two more months to see a little more of India. He laughed and said, "I know what you are going to see—donkeys, dust and doctors."

The next morning, I was so sick that I had to ask the hotel for a doctor. The prescribed antibiotics made me feel a little better, but over the next two months

I often suffered from diarrhea, because something in the Indian food didn't agree with me.

Yona bought airline tickets and we left, a few days later, to Bangalore on our way to Sathya Sai Baba in Puttaparthi. Our hotel in Bangalore was very basic and when we wanted to do our practice before going to bed, we found out that our room was next to a movie theatre; we had to do our meditation accompanied by "bang, bang, pow, pow!!!" and loud music. This was completely different from the quiet ashram in Rishikesh. We were back in the real world.

Somebody told us that Sai Baba was not in Puttaparthi, but in Whitefield, a suburb of Bangalore. We went there by taxi. There was a big crowd and we were able to just get a glimpse of him, seated under a big tent. Because the accommodation in Whitefield was full, people advised us go to Puttaparthi, because Sai Baba was moving there soon.

That afternoon we arrived in Puttaparthi and it looked very beautiful with the sculptured arch at the entrance, the clean street and the big buildings, richly decorated with statues and painted in pastel colors; it looked like heaven on earth. The ashram itself though didn't have that quality. The people in charge were very unfriendly and we had to put a lot of pressure on them before we were given a place to stay. We got a two-room apartment with a kitchen and a bathroom.

The apartment was terribly filthy, with black mold everywhere and there wasn't any furniture. We had to buy mattresses in the market outside the ashram, and also bedcovers, because the mattresses were not new. We purchased a lot of cleaning material and worked hard to make the place livable. In the evening we discovered that the kitchen for westerners was closed and that food was served in a huge, smelly and dirty hall, crawling with cockroaches. I really couldn't enter there without becoming nauseous, so the next few weeks I mainly lived on cookies, bread and bananas.

There wasn't a special place for yoga and meditation, so we spent most of the time in the room, where it was very hot. Outside the ashram we found a bookstore, where the first book that caught my attention was *Living with the Himalayan Masters* by Swami Rama. I bought it and spent the next few days reading. This book made me completely forget where I was.

Sai Baba arrived at the end of the week and the atmosphere in the ashram changed completely. A big crowd accompanied him and we had to share our apartment with two more ladies. One of them knew everything about the ashram and taught us how to survive in this crowded place.

Every morning and afternoon there was darshan. Sai Baba walked around a big square in front of his house, to meet with his devotees. The system of crowd control developed by the ashram people was perfect. Men and women were separated and half an hour before darshan everybody had to line up, sitting on the floor in single file rows. The first person in the line had to draw a number from a hat and that number indicated the order in which the rows could enter the darshan square.

It was a very special sensation to be part of a crowd of thousands of people, concentrating on one tiny man in an orange robe. Often after darshan, I stayed to meditate and that was wonderful. It was as if the whole crowd was supporting me with their prayers.

At every darshan, I took the letters with me, hoping that I could hand them over to Sai Baba, but he was always too far away. I was very interested in his miracles and tried to observe his hands all the time. Although I could see that he moved them in a special way, he was so far away that I didn't see anything miraculous.

Most of the time the weather was hot and sunny, but every now and then tropical rainstorms arrived, transforming the ashram roads into little rivers. We were asked to be very careful because there were dangerous snakes like cobras around.

One afternoon, when the rain fell in buckets, one of my roommates came home and said, "Go to the darshan square. Baba is walking in the rain and he doesn't get wet!"

This was my chance to see a miracle, so I rushed to the square and waited under a big umbrella. The square was completely empty and Sai Baba was nowhere to be seen. Just when I thought that this miracle business was pure nonsense and wanted to go back to the room, the door opened and Sai Baba came out, all by himself, without an umbrella to protect him from the heavy rain. He walked straight to the place where I stood, together with a few other people. He was wearing a silk orange robe on which every drop of rain would make a stain, but not a drop of water was falling, either on his robe, or on his afro-styled hair. Only his feet and the seam of his robe were wet, because he had to walk through the puddles.

I couldn't believe what I saw and cleaned my glasses a few times because I thought that something was wrong with my eyes. I pinched myself because I wanted to be sure that what I saw was real and not a kind of delusion. When he walked past me at a distance of maybe four meters, I clearly saw that the rain stopped in midair about 50 centimeters from his hair and body. It was as if he was walking within an invisible bubble. Seeing this, everything I

June Gable with Swami Rama in Rishikesh.

The Master leads the way.

Swami Rama at Hansda Ashram, Nepal.

June Gable with Nepalese children.

June Gable in conversation with Dr. S. N. Agnihotri
at Hansda Ashram, Nepal.

Dr. A. P. Singh at his clinic near
Hansda Ashram, Nepal.

June Gable today.

The young
Shri Roshan
Lal.

Dr. Sunandabai

Swami
Rama as a
young man.

Swami Rama meditating on the banks of the Naramada River when he was known as Patti Wale Baba.

Swami Rama when he was known as Bhole Baba.

Swami Rama (center) with devotees at
Sadhana Mandir Ashram.

Shri Roshan Lal (left) with Swami Rama at HIHT.

Dr. Renu Kapoor's father Prof. Radhey Shyam Tandon with Swami Rama at the Kanpur airport.

Mrs. Maya Tandon, Dr. Renu Kapoor (center), and Swami Rama in Minneapolis.

Swami Rama in kirtan playing the harmonium.

Dr. Renu Kapoor and her husband Shri Manoj Kapoor at the Himalayan Institute, Honesdale, Pennsylvania, USA.

Dr. Renu Kapoor with Swami Rama in Honesdale, Pennsylvania.

Swami Rama after his tennis game at Honesdale with Dr. Renu Kapoor standing behind him.

A young Shri Mehrotra greeting Swami Rama with
his son Rupesh in his arms.

Shri Mehrotra (far left) seeing Swamiji off at Kanpur.

Swami Rama with some of the Kanpur disciples
including Shri Mehrotra (far left).

Shri Mehrotra (second from left) with Swami Rama
in Rishikesh.

Judea (Hema's daughter) and her little miracle
of Sai Baba.

The
wedding
of Hema's
son
Martijn
in Japan.

Hema (far right) and friends in Sadhana
Mandir Ashram.

Hema as the soupcook in Honesdale.

Hema in Sadhana Mandir Ashram.

"The look of incredible love .... that went straight to
my heart." Hema De Munnik

The view of the Ganga in front of
Sadhana Mandir Ashram.

had ever learned in school and university, all logical and scientific thinking, became relative. Now I had to admit that miracles can really happen; I had seen it with my own eyes.

Yona had gone shopping that afternoon and when she came home I told her about what she had missed. Talking about miracles, we regretted that we never saw Swami Rama perform these things, although we knew from books and stories that he had done them in the past. Then during our conversation, it suddenly dawned on me that when we were in the ashram, something had happened that could be considered nothing less than a miracle.

When I met Yona for the first time and we agreed to travel together, she told me that she could only join me if her ankle was not giving her trouble. A few months earlier she had hurt herself badly and had to take rest for a long time before she was able to walk again. She still had to wear bandages and the pain wasn't completely gone. One morning, in the ashram in Rishikesh, she slipped in the bathroom, hurting the same ankle. She cried for help and we supported her to her bed. She was very much in pain and some ladies gave her a rescue remedy and homeopathic medicine.

That morning Swami Rama was scheduled to lecture. She didn't want to miss it, so we carried her to the meditation room and tried to make her as comfortable as possible by putting cushions under her leg and foot. She was still suffering from pain when after the lecture, Swami Rama noticed her and asked, "What's this?" Yona showed him her swollen ankle and said, "It's the second time already, Swamiji." Swami Rama said calmly, "It's nothing, get up and walk!" Yona objected, "I can't Swamiji." "Yes you can," said Swami Rama and helped her up. "Now walk," he said, and Yona walked without feeling any pain. "Take a day of rest and keep your foot in the Ganga; the swelling will go away soon," he said and walked away.

I was standing next to Yona when this happened, but it never crossed my mind that I was witnessing a miraculous healing. It was done in such a casual and inconspicuous way, that nobody noticed anything special. Even Yona said later that she maybe overreacted and that the pain might not have been that bad.

That afternoon in Sai Baba's ashram, we concluded that Swami Rama had indeed performed a miracle on her, because after the incident her ankle was completely healed and she didn't need bandages anymore. This shows that miracles are sometimes hard to recognize, because our rational mind only accepts what we think is logical.

Finally, after almost three weeks, the day came when the first person in my row drew number one and I could sit in the front row during darshan. Sai Baba slowly passed by and accepted my letters with a smile. I was glad that he didn't throw them back, like he sometimes did with other people's letters.

My mission accomplished, we could continue our journey. We were glad, because both of us felt that we didn't belong in this ashram and that Sai Baba was not our guru. I was grateful though for having seen him perform a miracle. Living in Sai Baba's ashram hadn't been easy for us, and in a letter to my relatives and friends in Holland I expressed some criticism about the atmosphere and the people. I mailed the letter in the ashram's post office and later found out that when it arrived in Amsterdam, only the first and the last page were readable. The other eight pages were empty, as if the words were washed away by water. Another of Sai Baba's miracles?

We went to Mysore by taxi. Having spent three weeks in a filthy apartment, we felt we deserved the best place on earth; so we took a room in a beautiful palace of the king of Mysore that had been transformed into a 5-star hotel. We enjoyed the quiet of the place and the high quality food that was served in a beautiful dining hall with live Indian classical music. We visited a lot of places in and around Mysore and even took an elephant ride and went tiger spotting.

Later we moved to Kovalam Beach in Kerala, where we met a young man who had just come back from a nearby ashram. He told us about a female saint and advised us to visit her. Although by now I had fully accepted Swami Rama as my guru, I was curious to know what a female saint looked like; so we took a boat through the picturesque backwaters and reached the ashram of Mata Amritanandamayi in the afternoon.

When we entered the ashram grounds, we were welcomed by a friendly young man, who said that he regretted very much that we hadn't come earlier, because Mother had just left for Australia and wouldn't be back before the end of the year.

It was a pity that we couldn't meet Amma personally, but we saw her personality reflected in her lovely disciples, who did everything to make us feel comfortable. We were given a bed in a dorm above the temple and attended yoga classes and meditation sessions on the roof. We participated in the Archana (chanting the 1000 names of Divine Mother) in the temple, where music, prayers and rituals were going on round the clock.

The atmosphere in this ashram was wonderful. There was a totally different energy than in Puttaparti. Everybody was full of love. I still remember the beauty of the place. The colors of the early morning sky, the pleasant temperatures, the smell of tropical flowers and the sound of temple bells and people praying and chanting at sunrise. I spent hours sitting there, grateful for everything that God was giving me.

Being in this ashram was like a warm bath. The music and rituals were beautiful, the people were loving and inspiring. Raised in a culture where God is considered a man and his church is also run by men, I never felt at ease in the Christian church. Here, for the first time in my life, I experienced the female aspect of the Divine and that was wonderful. It felt like a homecoming.

After a few weeks, Yona decided to continue her journey towards Sri Lanka, and I went to Cochin along with Elizabeth, a lady I met in the ashram. We stayed again in a palace hotel. It was very old and had been built by Dutch colonists. We did some sightseeing, saw a Kathakali performance and went to a temple festival with beautifully decorated elephants and deafening music.

By now it was already December and my time in India was almost over. I spent the last week in Delhi, visiting places like the Bahai Lotus Temple and Mahatma Gandhi's cremation place. I also took time to prepare myself for going home, back to the cold in Amsterdam, to my family and friends, and, after Christmas, to my former life in Curacao. I brought home lots of things—books, saris, gifts, pictures and an incredible amount of stories and experiences. It was good that I had written more than 10 letters. Now my relatives and friends were informed and warned that I had changed.

Transformation: Phase 2

Upon returning to Curacao, there were many books to read and practices to do. Four times a week I went to the yoga school for hatha and joints and glands, and three times a day I did japa and meditation. In between I practiced relaxation, pranayama and other exercises that I had learnt in India.

It wasn't easy to live alone. I still missed my partner, but I wasn't as depressed as when I left for India. The yoga practices and the support from friends in the meditation group, and from my daughter and son-in-law helped me start a new life.

I expected a lot from the new mantra, but soon found out that it didn't make much difference to the depth of my meditation. It was like the year before. Real meditation only happened every now and then, and I didn't know why. When it happened, it was so wonderful and easy that I was convinced I had found the key to get into it; but the next day this key didn't work anymore and I couldn't concentrate at all.

Sometimes I became impatient and blamed the mantra. "I know this mantra from my childhood, so it must be an easy one, something for children or for real beginners," I thought. "Next time I see Swami Rama, I'll ask him for a new mantra, one that is more powerful." Sometimes I tried other mantras or went back to soham, but that too didn't help.

What had changed though was my state of mind. I felt better about myself and had more positive feelings towards life than before. I also felt closer to God and was grateful that I had found a teacher who would help me with my spiritual development. The feelings of intense loneliness that had accompanied me since my early childhood were gone. For the first time in my life, I felt happy and satisfied without needing a partner to make me feel complete.

After some time, I began to hear a humming sound during my practice. I checked the refrigerator, the fan and other outside noises before I realized that the sound was inside my own head. I had read about the OM sound in Paramahamsa Yogananda's book and wondered if this could be it. I began to like the sound; sometimes it was so loud that I felt I could lean against it, for support while practicing.

I met Masterji, a music teacher from India and took lessons from him. I told him that I was interested in learning to play the harmonium, but couldn't sing. He said, "Yes, yes, I'll teach you ragas." I liked his classes very much and began to understand and appreciate Indian music. Masterji encouraged me to practice singing scales (alankars) and I discovered that my voice wasn't as bad as I had thought.

Although these were happy days, there was one big, dark cloud hanging over my head. I had to become a yoga teacher and establish a Himalayan Institute, but didn't have the faintest idea how to do this.

In June of 1992, after a long and complicated journey, I arrived in Honesdale, Pennsylvania. I flew from Curacao to Aruba, then to Miami, to Newark and finally reached the Scranton-Wilkesbarre airport, in the evening. Gopala picked me up and drove me to the Himalayan Institute. There he dropped me with my luggage in front of the double doors of the woman's wing and told me that my room was number 14.

My first impression of the Institute wasn't very positive. I saw long hallways like in a hospital, and the women's wing smelled like my grandmother's nursing home. My room though was nice, with old fashioned furniture and a light blue carpet. There wasn't an attached bathroom, so I had to go down the hall to find one. The hall was very dark and there were only doors with numbers. When I saw a lady dressed in white coming towards me, I wanted to introduce myself and ask her where the bathroom was, but I didn't get the chance. She seemed very upset when I addressed her and hissed, "Silence!"

I wondered what I had done wrong and doubted if this Institute was the right place for me. It wasn't as wonderful as the people I had met in India wanted me to believe. It looked more like a nunnery or even worse, like a mental hospital. Tired and confused, I went back to my room, urinated in the washbasin and went to bed!

In the morning I woke up late, still exhausted from the long journey. I felt as if I could sleep for weeks. Now there was light in the hallway and I immediately found the bathroom and the shower room. It was only a few steps away from where I had met the lady in white.

Compared with the cold shower of the night before, meeting with the other people in the dining room was like a warm bath. Thank God! The Institute wasn't as bad as it had seemed. Darlene Clarke, the person in charge of the Self Transformation Program (STP), gave me a friendly welcome and it wasn't long before I felt perfectly at home.

The five months I spent in Honesdale were like a rollercoaster ride. It started slowly, with the

STP program. I enjoyed the classes immensely and explored every niche and corner of the huge building. This was the first time in my life that I was living in a community of like-minded people and I felt like a fish in water. I made many new friends, participated in the hatha classes and attended all the lectures.

After a month, it was decided that I should work in the Combined Therapy department (CRX), where people came for treatment of various diseases. I met with the patients and joined them during their hatha classes in the morning. The teacher was Margo, a wonderful lady from Canada. After a few classes, she told me that she was going to India and that I had to fill in for her. I was shocked, my heart almost stopped beating. How could I do this? I had never taught hatha yoga. How could I teach people with so many specific physical problems?

I was so upset that I couldn't sleep that night. I prayed to the Lord to help me in this difficult situation. During the last class given by Margo, I made as many notes as I could and wrote down precise instructions in English. I decided to copy Margo's classes as far as possible.

The evening before my first hatha class for the CRX patients, I put the whole program on paper as if planning a lecture. I just had to look at my paper to know what to say. Teaching wasn't new to me. I had done it for more than 35 years. I learnt it when I was just a teenager in Teacher Training College, and after my graduation, I taught a few years in a primary school. After my University training as a psychologist, I lectured in psychology for 17 years and facilitated countless training sessions and workshops. I even taught a summer course in a college in New York City, but this was going to be my first class in hatha yoga for CRX patients and I was scared to death of making a mistake.

It was good that I knew the patients already and was aware of their specific problems. With the help of my papers, the first class went smoothly. After five minutes, it felt as if I had never done anything other than teach hatha yoga in English. Halfway through the class, the door opened and Swami Rama entered. "Is she a good teacher?" he asked the patients. "Yes," they said. He told me to continue and stayed for a few minutes. "You're doing fine," he said before he left. From that moment, I began to enjoy teaching hatha. It wasn't as hard as I thought and the students were great and forgave me my halting English and my heavy Dutch accent.

In addition to teaching hatha, I was asked to become a biofeedback therapist. I knew biofeedback from the time I studied at the university in the 1960s, but at that time there weren't any computers. Now I needed to learn how to operate a computer, something I hadn't done before, because in my college only secretaries were allowed to touch them.

The biofeedback therapist training was given by Kathy. After a few classes in which she taught us something about the theoretical background, she said, "By the way, I leave for India tomorrow." And to me she said, "You'll have your first patient on Monday." Again my heart stood still. How could I work with a patient when I didn't even know how to turn on a computer?

Dr. Clarke showed me a few things about the procedure, and said not to worry, because it was very easy. I wasn't so sure and on Monday morning I entered the biofeedback room with trembling knees. To my relief, I saw that my first patient was Gus Gatto, who happened to be very familiar with biofeedback and computers, because he was a regular patient of CRX. Instead of a patient, he became my teacher and I'm still grateful for his help.

As soon as I felt comfortable teaching hatha and doing biofeedback with CRX patients, another challenge was put before me. The lady who worked in the CRX office told me that she was leaving and that I had to do her job. This meant that I had to answer the phone and do office work. These were things I had never done before, and again I was very scared. Swami Rama was really testing my limits.

Answering the phone, finding out what people's problems were, and what kind of help they wanted from Combined Therapy was very hard, because I often couldn't understand their American English. Filling in insurance forms was worse, an absolutely impossible task. So this time, I said, "Sorry, I can't do this, please find someone else who can do this job." To my relief, one of the CRX patients happened to be a doctor's assistant and was willing to stay on to help me with the office work.

These experiences made me grow a lot. It seemed that Swami Rama was giving me things to do that I was very afraid of. Outside the Institute I could avoid them, but here, I was forced to face my anxieties one by one, and find ways to overcome them. The presence and support of Swami Rama made a huge difference. When I met him in the hallway, he often put his arm around me and asked, "How's my daughter doing today?" He was very loving and said that I was doing a great job in CRX. This really gave me wings to soar up high.

Once, when I had a question for Swami Rama, I wrote it on a piece of paper and gave it to the receptionist. When I walked back to the dining room, a person whom I had never seen before, approached me and out of the blue gave me the answer to my question. Was this a miracle? I also began to notice that many of my wishes were instantly fulfilled, in rather unexpected ways.

For Guru Purnima, I wanted to wear Indian clothes, but hadn't brought any with me. I was just thinking how much I regretted this, when I saw somebody put a beautiful light blue salwar kameez in the Goodwill charity box. It was exactly my size. In the gift shop, I often looked at an expensive golden pendant with the OM sign, regretting that I couldn't afford to buy it. One of the CRX patients, a schoolteacher from New York City, put a small package in my hands, before she went home. When I opened it, it was the OM pendant that I wanted so badly. To this day I'm still wearing it.

Next to my work in CRX, I spent time practicing hatha and meditation, reading interesting books, and studying yoga philosophy. I loved to browse in the bookstore and purchased many books to take home to Curacao. One day, when I left the bookstore with my arms loaded with books, Swamiji saw me and asked, "Are you reading all of these?" When I nodded my head, he said, "Don't read, write! Every day you should write about the goal and purpose of your life and what you do to attain it." He walked away and didn't give me time to tell him that I was already doing this since April 1991.

At the low point of my crisis, the day after I left my partner, I discovered that it gave me relief to start the day with writing a few lines. It was like composing my mind on paper. Every morning I tried to answer the same questions:

What is the goal of my life?
What am I going to do today towards attaining that goal?

And in the evening I answered the question:
What did I do today towards attaining this goal?

I followed this procedure for many years and accumulated a long row of writing books on my bookshelf, filled with answers to these questions. It might seem silly to answer the same question over and over again, but every morning, when I sat down to write, it was as if I was contemplating this question for the first time. This exercise has been very helpful to me. It gave structure to my thinking and it also improved my writing skills.

At the end of October, I decided that it was time to go home. I knew the basics of yoga philosophy and felt comfortable teaching hatha. In Honesdale, I had met Erwin Jamaloodin from Curacao, and learned that Swami Rama had asked him to look for a building to start a Himalayan Institute. I had no idea how that had worked out, but I knew that Swami Rama was going to help me, like he did from the day I met him.

I arrived in Curacao on November 2nd. My daughter Judea and son-in law Elijah were waiting for me at the airport; I immediately noticed that they were hiding something from me. I was a bit irritated because they had never written to me while I was in Honesdale and hadn't answered my letters. I also couldn't understand why they were giggling all the time and behaving like silly teenagers. When we got home, they finally told me the great news — they were expecting a baby! Judea was 3½ months pregnant and in very good health. This was the best news I had ever gotten. I had already given up hope of becoming a grandmother; now, with Sai Baba's grace, Judea was going to have a child. This was a wonderful surprise.

Another surprise came when I went through the mail that had come during my absence. There, I found an invitation for the official opening of the Himalayan

Institute of Curacao. I didn't know that Swami Rama's Indian students, together with Erwin Jamaloodin, had already rented a building and established the Institute. Suddenly all my worries were gone. I was able to start teaching at the Himalayan Institute of Curacao the very next week. Thank you Swamiji, you are great!

Teaching in Curacao wasn't as easy as working in Honesdale. Curacao is a small island; as it already had a yoga school with good teachers, I began to doubt if there were enough people interested in yoga to make our new Institute a success. But after a few quiet weeks, more students signed up to participate in the activities of the new center. I taught hatha classes for adults and children and on Saturday mornings I assisted with preparing take-away vegetarian meals. There were cooking classes, study groups, stress management courses and sometimes kirtan and group meditation sessions. On Sunday afternoons, we watched one of Swamiji's videos. Doing selfless service in the new Himalayan Institute was a demanding but pleasant job.

One day, when some of my most dedicated hatha students didn't show up, I was bewildered and couldn't understand why. One of the students told me that the Roman Catholic Church, to which most people in Curacao belong, advised people not to go to yoga classes. The priest had said this in his sermon during Sunday mass. I knew the priest and liked him; so I went to see him and asked him what the problem was. He said that yoga is like peeking into God's kitchen. You shouldn't do that, it's impolite. You shouldn't be curious about what God is going to put on the table for you. We had a long conversation, but I couldn't convince him that yoga is beneficial for body and mind, and that it deepens your faith and trust in God, and can make you a better Catholic.

In April, Judea gave birth to a beautiful baby boy and called him Lumukanda, which means 'the eternal immortal.' She stayed with me the first few weeks, and I loved to take care of her and her little miracle of Sai Baba.

Soon after this, I went back to Honesdale for further study and practice. Although by now I knew a lot more about yoga philosophy than before, there were still many things I didn't understand. I was especially puzzled by the way Swami Rama explained the four functions of mind. As a lecturer in psychology, I considered myself an expert in cognitive matters. In the University, I had made an in-depth study of the theory of Piaget. When Swami Rama spoke of the mind, I didn't recognize anything. In the beginning I resisted the new information and put it aside as something I would sort out later. But now, I wanted to find out what Swamiji really meant when he spoke about the four functions of mind: manas, chitta, buddhi and ahamkara.

I also wanted more clarity about the status of my meditation. Why didn't it work most of the time, and why did it feel as if nothing was happening? It often looked more like a wrestling match with my monkey mind and I wondered if I was doing something wrong. But I also noticed that feelings of self-acceptance were rising up, because of my meditation. One morning, I wrote in my diary, "O.k., I'm not a good meditator, but I can always try to do it to the best of my ability, and I should not be discouraged when my expectations are not met." Slowly I began to look at meditation more as a developmental process than as an achievement to be proud of, and discovered that my ego was the main stumbling block.

The second summer in Honesdale was different, but equally wonderful. I worked with Dr. Clarke in

CRX and we had many patients. There was a Congress with famous speakers like Deepak Chopra and David Frawley, and many distinguished guests wanted their stress profile recorded. The insecurities and anxieties of the previous year were mostly gone now, and my mind was calm and quiet. I felt relaxed and at ease in this job and enjoyed working with the patients and with Dr. Clarke.

After work, I tried to practice hatha, meditation and japa. When I met Swamiji, he was very loving and I was less shy than the year before. One time, I complained about my meditation and he said, "It takes time, keep practicing." I told him that I loved to listen to the OM sound and he said, "Don't pay attention to it; it's not important. Listen to the mantra only." Then I asked him if he could give me a Sanskrit name. He answered, "I'll think about it and let you know." That evening, my meditation was much better. I felt light, as if the air around me was supporting my body, and that the thoughts that were present in my mind were like seagulls flying around my head and didn't bother me. I could concentrate on the mantra and stay with it.

The way Swamiji was showering love on everybody, and the non-judgmental and respectful attitude he showed towards the many people who came to see him at the Institute, became a kind of model for me. This was how I too wanted to behave towards patients and other people. Knowing that he was nearby, made every type of work light and joyful, even doing dishes or sweeping stairwells.

On the morning of Guru Purnima, I met Swamiji in the hallway. He blessed me by putting his hands on my head and told me that my Sanskrit name would be Hema, mother/daughter of the Himalayas or mother/daughter of the snows. When he noticed my bewilderment, he said, "It's a beautiful energy

and will make you very happy." But I wasn't happy
at all. Actually I was very disappointed. I love Indian
names, but I had never heard of Hema before. In
Holland, Hema is the name of a chain of inexpensive
department stores, like Walmart or K-mart in the U.S.
The word Hema also reminded me of the time my
teenage daughter used to call me from afar, "Hey Ma!
Can you do this or that for me?" I was always very
irritated when she said that, and sometimes answered,
"I'm not Hema or any other department store, do it
yourself."

This new name was really a blow to my ego. How
could I tell my friends and relatives at home that from
now on they would have to call me Hema, the store
famous for its warm sausages? Having a guru and
changing your name is already something not done
in Holland and this name surely would make people
laugh at me. Although my friends at the Institute liked
my new name, and started using it immediately, I was
very unhappy with it. In the evening I met Swamiji
at the pond. "And how are you doing with your new
name?" he asked. I said, "Swamiji, you've given me
a lot of homework. In Dutch, Hema means K-mart."
Swamiji laughed, and said that in India it's the name
of a famous actress and movie star. He also said that
I should read the Ramayana to find out who Hema
really is, and while walking away, he added, "You'll
be surprised."

The book, *The Valmiki Ramayana Retold in Verse*
by Swami Rama had just come out. The next few
days, I read it to find out who this Hema was. When
I learnt that she was a celestial nymph, living in a
cave, beautifully decorated with gemstones, where
she entertained the gods, I felt better about my name.
I certainly could relate to this Hema and wondered
what else Swami Rama knew about my past.

When a message was posted that people who wanted to help in the hospital in India could sign up, I thought about it and asked Swamiji if I could be of any use. "Not yet," he said. "You're too expensive." I still don't understand what he meant, because I've always been financially independent.

The work in the Center in Curacao took all my energy. It was a busy, but rewarding job. A regular group of people attended the morning hatha classes and the 6-week stress management courses were a success. Some of the students wanted individual hatha sessions and stayed on after they had finished the course. Despite the hard work, the financial situation of the Center was of concern, because of the very high rent we had to pay for the building. The vegetarian meals we sold on Saturday morning were really needed to make extra money.

In January 1994, I went to Japan, where my son Martijn married his Japanese girlfriend Fumiko. After the wedding, I did a bit of sightseeing and stayed overnight in a monastery in Koyasan, a picturesque mountain village full of temples. In the monastery I participated in a morning meditation ritual. It was interesting, but a bit scary, because I didn't understand what the monks were shouting and why they were moving their swords in a ferocious manner, as if they were fighting demons. I was the only visitor in the room and at the end of the ceremony, I was invited to come to the front, and asked to bend over the fire. After a firm blow on my back with a sword, I could leave the room. It was an interesting experience, but I prefer the morning prayers in Honesdale.

My meditation had its usual ups and downs, but now the way I approached it had changed. My expectations had become more realistic. I wasn't aiming at spectacular images and supernatural sounds anymore, but discovered very subtle changes in my personality instead. As a teacher in school and college, I always had to evaluate and judge my students as well as myself. Now I learned that communicating with people and looking at myself in a positive and non-judgmental way was much better. I took my practice very seriously and tried to sit for meditation every day at the same time. I discovered that for me the best time to meditate was 3:30 a.m., right after waking up from deep sleep. When I woke up between 4:00 a.m. and 6:00 a.m., I often came out of dream sleep, and then my mind was filled with images and thoughts, which made it difficult to concentrate.

Doing pranayama, sun salutations and asanas before going to the Center at 7:15 in the morning was important, because I wanted to stay balanced and fit. Compared to a few years earlier, I felt more contented and peaceful. Sometimes during meditation, I felt a terrible longing for something. It wasn't an earthly thing; I can best describe it as longing for direct contact with the Divine. I craved to be united with all there is. This longing which had begun in my teenage years had now become a lot stronger.

During my crisis in 1991, I developed the habit of talking to God when I encountered a problem that I couldn't manage. Often I immediately got a response, and sometimes, I even heard a voice giving me instructions. When I asked Swamiji where this voice was coming from, he answered, "It's your own voice. All the answers are already inside of you." One day, in the fall of 1993, I complained to God that I felt such a big distance between me and the Divine. I literally said, "Please Lord, do something that brings me closer to You." Half an hour later, I received a letter from the U.S. with terrible accusations against Swamiji. It hit me hard, but I knew I had asked for it, and immediately sat down to ask the Lord for strength and wisdom to handle this situation. I realized that Swamiji would always be my God-given guru, so although I was very sad and confused, my faith in God and in Swamiji weren't influenced by this information.

During 1993-1994, there were more problems to deal with. At the Center we had to struggle hard to make ends meet and my daughter's marriage fell apart. Shortly after Lumukanda's first birthday, Judea decided to separate from her husband and return to Holland. I agreed that this was the best solution for her and for her son. I was grateful to have been with Luma during the first year of his life.

My third summer in Honesdale was different, because Swamiji was in India and Dr. Clarke was in Boston. However, being with my guru brothers and sisters was wonderful. Panditji gave me a Gayatri practice to do and I spent a lot of time in the meditation room, doing japa. In the morning, I worked in the kitchen and after lunch in the bookstore, which I enjoyed very much.

Back in Curacao, I learnt that the Himalayan Institute had to vacate its building because the house was going to be sold. This was a big problem because an affordable place was hard to find. We had to raise more money, so I taught many hatha classes, gave yoga therapy and biofeedback sessions, cleaned the house and maintained the garden. This was often a bit too much for me and I thought that it would be good if some of my most advanced students could help me with teaching hatha. With this in mind, I organized an intensive hatha training program for a small group of students in the fall of 1994. In the spring of 1995, Dave Gorman came from Honesdale to put the finishing touches.

My life was very busy, because next to my work in the Himalayan Institute, I was helping my friend Gerda from the meditation group, who was in a wheelchair because of a spinal cord lesion. I kept her company in the afternoon when her nurse had gone home, and if one of her nurses didn't show up, I took her place. Never in my life had I worked with sick or handicapped people. I always stayed away from hospitals, sickness and death because I was afraid of them. But with Gerda, who was a very spiritual and wise woman and a dear friend, I felt honored when she asked me to help her. With a group of friends, we took her to the beach for a swim once a week and I assisted her when she taught watercolor painting and other activities to a group of children.

Looking back, I can see that the years 1993 to 1995 were a time of serious testing. Since 1991, I had tried to concentrate fully on my yoga and meditation practice and on doing selfless service in the Center. In the beginning, it was a joyful activity and I always felt supported and inspired by Swamiji, but by 1994 it had become more and more of a burden. I didn't have as much energy as before and was often tired. The communication with Erwin, the director of the Center, was problematic and the prospect of losing the building was discouraging. My health also deteriorated. The gynecologist discovered a pre-cancerous lesion and told me that this couldn't be treated in Curacao.

In my personal life it looked as if bad habits from the past were making a comeback. The four primitive fountains often overpowered me. Every day I had to struggle against eating too much or eating the wrong type of food; against going to bed too late and waking up after my practice time. When another Mr. Wonderful crossed my path I fell back into my old habits of sexual fantasies and unrest. Curacao had a big problem with drug-related crimes and I felt more and more unsafe in my little house, where the doors and windows couldn't be properly locked. My anxiety increased after my friends from the meditation group were attacked and robbed in their ow bedroom. My small studio was the only place in the vhole area that hadn't been visited by burglars. During my practice, I often concentrated more on the door and the sounds outside, than on my mantra.

I felt I needed Swamiji's advice and decided to write him a letter. One of my Indian friends was going to Rishikesh, and I gave her the letter to be delivered personally to Swamiji. I wrote that I loved to live on the beautiful island of Curacao, but that lately there were a few things that I needed help with. About my personal problems, I wrote that I often failed in maintaining a yogic lifestyle and that I didn't know how to improve communication with Erwin.

In the summer of 1995, the situation in the Center became worse. I had to teach in three different locations—the dirty porch of an empty villa next to a noisy construction site, a room in a martial arts school with a soft and unstable floor, and a room in a children's daycare center. There weren't many students interested in yoga classes in this type of Himalayan Institute.

Because I didn't get a direct answer from Swamiji, I decided to sign up for the tour to India in September. I could then meet him in person and ask for advice. In June I went to Honesdale together with some of my hatha students from Curacao. It was wonderful to do the STP program together with them.

Like the year before, I worked in the kitchen and in the bookstore, but my health was problematic. I took homeopathic medicine and started a Maha Mrityunjaya practice to get some relief. I had to stay in my room for more than two weeks because of a bad cold. That was a kind of cleansing I needed badly.

One day, during my meditation, what I had to do became clear. In a letter to Swamiji I wrote that I wanted to take a year off from the work in Curacao and asked if I could stay in the ashram in Rishikesh to do sadhana. I also told him about my health problem that couldn't be treated in Curacao. Not long after that, I knew I had to leave Curacao for good. I had spent a wonderful period of eight years there and had gone through a complete transformation, but now I felt that I needed to move on. I was very relieved when this decision was made. It was hard to sell my car and most of my belongings and to say farewell to my dear friends and students, but I practiced nonattachment and happily looked forward to the next phase in my life.

Transformation: Phase 3

On my first day in India, I visited Swamiji at the hospital together with Sharon Wilkinson. I was shocked when I saw him. He looked very old and weak, completely different from how he had been two years earlier; but he radiated love like always. "I'm so glad that you have come," he said to us many times. The night before, on the plane to Delhi, I had thanked the Lord for having given me a guru who still had a body, but when I saw him, I knew he was going to leave us. Suddenly, it was as if he cast a magic spell on me; my thoughts were wiped out and my mind became totally blank, as if a door had been closed. We were shown around the new hospital building and saw people working hard to finish the construction of the Medical College that was to be opened shortly.

In the ashram, we stayed in the last room of the beautiful new building on the ground floor. One afternoon, when I opened the screen door, there was a long black snake behind it, swallowing a frog. I called Tiwariji, the gardener, and instead of being afraid and running away, he sat down near the snake, took out his mala and started repeating his mantra. "This is very auspicious," he said. "Lord Shiva has come." After the snake had swallowed the frog, it silently slid away between the bushes, never to be seen again.

The tour with the American group was interesting. I'm glad to have had the opportunity to visit Gaya and

Bodh Gaya, the holy shrines of Buddhism. When we were in Benares, I got a phone call from Judea with the news that my former partner in Curacao had died of a stroke and that Fumiko, my daughter-in-law, had had a miscarriage. This was sad news. I wanted to share it with Pandit Rajmani, but he was busy with other people. I felt very much alone with my grief.

The next day the group visited a small temple, beautifully decorated with light blue tiles. Pandiji told us that this temple was often visited by people to get relief from sadness and grief, just what I badly needed. I took a moment to sit down and asked the deity if he/she could take the feelings of sadness away from me. That was instantly done, and the rest of the day I felt better.

We also visited a town with a famous temple. We were asked to leave our shoes in a nearby house and had to walk barefoot through the dirty streets to the temple. This was very hard for me. I'm not good at walking without shoes; having to walk through dirt and cow dung was a nightmare. In the temple it was wet and slippery and it took all of my attention to keep from falling. I didn't see anything of the temple except for the floor, and was relieved when I made it through the excursion without breaking a leg or hip and was able to put my shoes back on.

While visiting this temple, a strange phenomenon took place inside my body and mind. A terrible anger started growing within me. I didn't know where it came from and why it was happening. It became so strong that I could hardly control myself. I was still fighting it when we visited a few other temples. I really didn't know what to do. When I saw a quiet Devi temple, I entered it and while I was restlessly pacing up and down, I prayed to Divine Mother, asking her to take this unbearable rage away from me. To my great relief she did! I've never been able to talk about these experiences because I found them too weird.

We visited a very special place with a cottage where Swami Rama had lived with his master Babaji. We found the tomb of Bhole Baba next to it. At that time I was puzzled, but later I learnt from Swami Veda Bharati that Swami Rama, during this lifetime, had taken another body. When we sat down to listen to a tantric master whom I couldn't understand, I closed my eyes, and then, what I always call the "Findhorn experience" happened again. I took off and was in heaven for some time. The impact of this experience was very strong and has stayed with me to this very day.

I spent the winter in the ashram teaching hatha, doing japa and meditation and singing the morning and evening prayers the way I had been taught in Honesdale. I liked the work very much because the guests were always very motivated. I also liked Prem, the ashram manager. We had a lot of fun together. If people were interested, we did kirtan and watched Swami Rama's lectures on video.

I didn't see much of Swamiji because he was busy in the hospital. One afternoon I got a phone call from Sharon. It was nice talking to her and at the end of the call I had to promise to give Swamiji a big hug from her. Exactly at that moment, Swamiji arrived by car and I overcame my shyness and said, "Swamiji, I promised Sharon Wilkinson to give you a big hug." Swamiji opened his arms and when we hugged I felt only bones under his red robe. It was like hugging a skeleton, and for a moment I was very disturbed. Then he made my mind go blank again. Apparently he didn't want me to worry about his health.

In March of 1996, my visa expired and I had to go back to Holland. Before I left, I asked Swamiji if I could return after the summer, and he said, "Of course, this is your home." I saw that he was very ill and asked, "Will you be here when I come back in September?" "Yes of course," he said, and he blessed me by touching my forehead.

I visited Honesdale and spent time with my friends in Curacao. The Himalayan Institute of Curacao had stopped its activities but some of my former students had started teaching hatha to their friends. I saw my physician who said that my condition had improved, but that there were still a few things to work on. I wrote in my diary that staying in India and doing the Maha Mrityunjaya practice had helped me a lot. I felt much better than I had felt a year earlier.

In the beginning of July, I returned to Holland, because I promised Swami Veda to help him with his program. When I met him in The Hague on the 13th of July, I immediately asked him how Swamiji was doing. He said that he had seen him just before he left India and that Swamiji looked much better. He had said, "Four more months." Swami Veda assumed that this meant that he would be cured after four months, but I wasn't so sure of this. I counted from the 13th of July and came up with the 13th of November, a date easy to remember because it was my ex-husband's birthday. Instinctively I knew that November 13th would be an important day and hoped that Swami Veda's interpretation was the right one.

Back in the ashram in September, I learnt that Swamiji had gone for a walk, which was good news; but when I wanted to see him a few days later, I was told that it wasn't possible because he had a slight fever. This reminded me of the day in May 1944, when I ran home immediately after school because my father was coming back from the hospital that day. When I arrived, my mother was very sad and told me that he hadn't come home because he had a slight fever. I still remember my disappointment. Since that day the words "slight fever" always trigger my tears, because I never saw my father again.

During my japa and meditation, many childhood memories, especially from when my father was dying of cancer, popped up. All my life, I had pushed them away because they were too painful and made me sad. But now I was 52 years older, and needed to learn to deal with them in a more mature way. It was as if Swamiji was teaching me not to panic and to worry like I did when I was a child.

The last week of September, Swamiji was able to see me. That morning he must have been in pain, because he was keeping a hot water bottle against his body, and his voice was very weak. His eyes were still radiating love, but I wrote in my diary that he looked as if he was already half gone. There were lots of questions I wanted to ask, but none of them came to my lips. I only asked for his blessings for my daughter. He said that the only thing I could do for her was to pray. Then he looked straight into my eyes and said, "Keep doing your practice and don't escape!" Those were his last words to me. I'll remember them always.

Back in the ashram, I knew that this was the last time that I had seen my guru in the body. But there was always that little spark of hope, that one day he would reverse the process of physical disintegration by his yogic power and stay with us forever. With a few people we went to Dehradun, to visit the ashram of Anandamayi Ma. It was like a museum, dusty and lifeless. The thought that in a couple of years, our ashram could become like that, made me upset and I prayed that this should never happen.

My friend Jutta arrived with the group from Germany. We had met a few years before in Honesdale and I visited her in Ahrensburg, where I took care of her house and garden while she was on vacation. Seeing her this time, I was worried. She looked different, puffed up and unhealthy. After cancer surgery in the hospital a year ago, Swamiji had asked her to come to India and stay for a longer time, to help Barb Bova with creating an Ayurvedic garden. She planned to stay for as long as her visa would permit, and then decide if she was going to settle in India permanently. I noticed that she wasn't as enthusiastic as before; apparently something was bothering her.

Elke was also part of this group. We liked each other and often spent time together. The morning of November 13th, she came crying to my room. In a dream she had seen Swamiji drowning in the Ganga. He waved at her and then disappeared below the waters. We were both very sad and went for a walk along the Ganga. We sat down to pray at a small temple on the other side of the barrage. The priest noticed our grief and performed a puja for us. We didn't understand much of it, but we hoped that this would make Swamiji's last hours a bit lighter. When we walked back to the ashram we felt better. We knew that the mortal aspect of Swamiji wasn't what we needed most. For us, he had always been much more than a body and we kept hoping that this wouldn't change.

The rest of the day was just like all other days. I felt calm and peaceful and my meditation in the evening went exceptionally well. The next morning, when I was teaching hatha in the meditation hall, the telephone in Swamiji's apartment upstairs was ringing continuously. I became irritated and wondered why there was nobody to answer the phone. Then someone came in and said that Swamiji had left his body the night before. Although we were prepared, it was still a blow. Almost everybody was in tears and we finished the class with a short meditation.

Prem said that there was a car going to the hospital and that I should go to say goodbye to Swamiji. I hesitated because all my life I had been afraid of things that had to do with death. I never dared to look at a dead body. I was afraid that I would become unwell and faint or wouldn't be able to control my emotions. But this time, something inside me said that I had to overcome my fears and go to see Swamiji, like everybody else.

In the car, memories of my father's funeral in August 1944 haunted me. I was six years old and had spent the summer with my aunt and uncle. One day, to my surprise, they dressed me up in my most beautiful clothes and took me to my home. My grandfather opened the door in a dark suit. I remember that I said, "Oh grandpa, you look so handsome! Are we having a party?" Inside the house everything looked different. The walls and windows were covered with black cloth. I hardly recognized my mother, completely dressed in black. She cried and took me to the living room where she showed me my father, who was lying in a coffin. When I saw his frozen face, I panicked and ran away. I went to the garden and hid in the scariest place I could think of, the coal shed, where big spiders lived. I threw myself on a heap of coal and screamed and cried my eyes out. It took a while before they found me. I was told to go inside, but I refused and screamed and shouted and kicked them against their shins. When they lifted me up, I banged my head against a branch of the maple tree and made a terrible scene. After some time my grandmother came. She cleaned me and tried to console me by saying that my father had gone to heaven above. To me, that seemed like the worst possible place to go to, because that was where bombs and burning airplanes were falling from. When I finally dared to go inside, I saw the coffin being carried out of the house by men dressed in black.

At the hospital campus, the room where Swamiji's body was kept was full. I managed to find a place behind other people, as far away from Swamiji's body as possible. I closed my eyes and tried to meditate. Repeating my mantra helped me to stay composed. After some time, I became more relaxed and found the courage to look at Swamiji's body. That was a very deep experience. It felt as if balm was being applied to long existing wounds. I stayed in the room and looked at Swamiji most of the day and night. Many people came in and put marigolds on Swamiji's body. In the evening only his face and feet were visible and the room was filled with the fragrance of flowers. I sat close to his body and felt all the fears haunting me since childhood melt away. This was one of Swamiji's greatest gifts to me.

The next day, I attended the cremation on the bank of the Ganga in Haridwar. That was an equally wonderful experience. I stood as close to the pyre as possible and felt that the heat and the flames were purifying me. With his energy, Swamiji gave me the strength to move on with my life in a more mature way than before.

My newly acquired fearlessness was immediately tested a few days after the cremation. I learnt that fast growing, incurable tumors had been found in Jutta's abdomen and that she had only a short time left to live. She asked me to be with her when she needed help; of course, I agreed. On the day of Swami Rama's bhandara, when thousands of people visited the hospital campus to remember Swamiji, Jutta was too sick to participate, but she could see everything from her chair on the roof of the guesthouse. I also didn't take part in the celebration because I was organizing transportation for Jutta's sister and niece who were on their way from Germany.

There wasn't a phone connection in the guesthouse and I had to walk to the village several times, right through the crowds who were arriving from all directions. I noticed that they weren't sad, like I expected when someone has died. Some of them were loud and quarrelsome and others, I felt, didn't behave properly. There was one elderly man who even looked happy. He was moving around as if he was a little drunk. I avoided looking at him because I was annoyed about his improper behavior. Later, I saw his photograph on the last page of Pandit Rajmani's pictorial biography of Swami Rama!

Postscript

After Swamiji left his body, my transformation has continued. It's going on to this very day. He's guiding me wherever I go. He supported me when I did selfless service in the pediatric ward of the Himalayan Hospital, and when I worked with the children on the hospital campus. He helped me write the book, *Bhole, Adventures of a Young Yogi,* about the childhood of a boy like Swami Rama.

In December 2006, I left India for good and moved to Putten. Swamiji's grace provided me with a wooden cabin in Putten (Holland), when I needed a private place to stay. A few months later my boxes arrived from India. In one of them I found the tape of my initiation and decided to listen to it once more, because I wanted to hear Baba's voice. To my great astonishment the mantra had changed. I didn't know what to think of it. Had I been repeating the wrong mantra all these years? When I was in Curacao and also in India, I had listened to this tape many times, but had never heard this mantra before. There was also something added to the visualization. I started to doubt my sanity and immediately called Kamal in India. She said, "Don't worry, he has done this before." It hasn't been easy to work with the new mantra. Every now and then the old one still comes up.

When a few years ago, the winter climate in Holland was turning out to be too hard for my ageing body, he directed me to Spain, to a town called La Vila Joyosa, a lovely place on the Costa Blanca, where the winters are mild. Here I continue to do my practice the way he taught me and live a quiet and contemplative life. Under his guidance, I keep working on myself and want to continue to do this until my last day in this body.

I am so grateful that after my search of more than 50 years and after having walked countless deadend streets, God finally gave me Swami Rama as a guru. He taught me how to love, how to live, and how to enjoy this wonderful life.

Putten/Villajoyosa, December 2011

Glossary

AHAMKARA   The sense of 'I-ness' or individuality, the ego

ARCHANA   Rite of worship

ASHTANGA YOGA   Yoga of eight limbs or steps, Raja Yoga

BABA   Literally father, honorific term for a wise or holy person

BHAGAVAD GITA   Song Divine, philosophical text , part of Mahabharata, the Hindu epic

BHANDARA   A feast that is open to all, in honor of yogis and renunciates

BHANG   Marijuana

BRAHMAN   The Supreme Being, Cosmic Self

BUDDHI   The discriminating faculty of the mind that makes decisions and judgments

CHARAN SPARSHA   Reverential obeisance to the feet of a holy person or elder

CHITTA   Storehouse of memories and experiences

DARSHAN   Literally sight, used when viewing something holy

DEEPAVALI OR DIWALI   Hindu Festival of lights celebrating the victory of good over evil

DOSA   South Indian pancake made from a rice-lentil batter

DURGA MANGAL   A festival in honor of the Divine Mother

GANGA DUSSEHRA Ten-day festival in veneration of the holy Ganges river

GAYATRI MANTRA Sacred Hindu mantra in praise of the solar deity

GURU BHAI OR BEHEN Guru brother or sister, disciples of the same guru

GURU CHAKRA Energy center just above the eyebrow center

HAVAN Fire ceremony

JANMASHTAMI FESTIVAL Celebrating the birth of Lord Krishna

JAPA Repetition of a mantra either mentally or aloud

KARVA CHAUTH A fast observed from sunrise to moonrise by women for the longevity of their husbands

KIRTAN Devotional singing with audience participation

MAHANTJI Head of an institution

MAHASAMADHI Voluntary act of dropping the body and being absorbed in the Supreme

MANAS Lower aspect of mind that imports and exports sensory stimuli

MRITYUNJAYA MANTRA Sacred Hindu mantra in praise of Lord Shiva used for protection and healing

NAGA SADHU Renunciate of a Shiva sect who is naked and smeared with ashes

NAGMANI Precious stone from a cobra's hood

NANAK SARAI Guest house on the HIHT campus for relatives of patients, named after Guru Nanak, the founder of the Sikh religion

NAVRATRI A festival of nine nights dedicated to worship of the Divine Mother

PANDAL A temporary tent-like structure for public ceremonies

PANDIT Scholar well versed in the religious scriptures, priest

PARAS Stone that changes base metals into gold

PATTI WALE BABA Leaf Baba

POORI Fried Indian bread

PRASAD Sanctified offering received in a temple or after a religious ritual

PRATIPADA The fourth day of the Diwali festival and the first day of the bright fortnight of the lunar month Kartik

RUDRAKSH Literally eye of Rudra (Shiva), a special seed used in rosaries for Shiva mantras

SADHAKA Spiritual practitioner

SALWAR KAMEEZ Indian dress comprising of pajamas and tunic

SAMOSA Fried pastry snack with a spicy filling

SARI A draped dress worn by Indian women

SATSANG Gathering for sharing of spiritual teachings

SHANKARACHARYA Head of a monastery established by the 8th century philosopher-saint of India, Adi Shankara

SHANTI HAVAN A fire ceremony for promoting peace

SHIV MAHIMNA STROTRA Sanskrit composition in praise of Lord Shiva

SHIVRATRI Night of Shiva, festival dedicated to worship of Lord Shiva

SHRAVAN Fifth lunar month of the Hindu calendar

SOHAM Generic mantra that resembles the sound of the in and out breaths

TABLA North Indian percussion music instrument

TANTRA VIDYA Science of Tantra, the philosophy of the play of male (Shiva) and female (Shakti) energies in the universe

TILAK   Mark applied to the forehead in religious rites

UPANISHADS   Philosophical section of the sacred Hindu scriptures called the Vedas

VALMIKI RAMAYANA   The Ramayana of Sage Valimiki, the epic story of Lord Rama

VEDANTA   Literally end portion of the Vedas, school of non-dual philosophy

VISHUDDHA CHAKRA   Energy center at throat

VISHWA SARA TANTRA   Tantric scriptural text

YUG DHARMA KYA HAI   Book title: *What is the Dharma (guiding principle) for the Age?*

Swami Rama

Swami Rama was born in the Himalayas in 1925. He was initiated by his master into many yogic practices. In addition, Swamiji's master sent him to other yogis and adepts of the Himalayas to gain new perspectives and insights into the ancient teachings. At the young age of 24 he was installed as the Shankaracharya of Karvirpitham in South India. Swamiji relinquished this position to pursue intense sadhana in the caves of the Himalayas. Having successfully completed this sadhana, he was directed by his master to go to Japan and to the West in order to illustrate the scientific basis of the ancient yogic practices. At the Menninger Foundation in Topeka, Kansas, Swamiji convincingly demonstrated the capacity of the mind to control so-called involuntary physiological parameters such as heart rate, temperature and brain waves.

Swamiji's work in the United States continued for 23 years and in this period he established the Himalayan International Institute of Yoga Science and Philosophy of the U.S.A. Swamiji became well recognized in the U.S. as a yogi, teacher, philosopher, poet, humanist and philanthropist. His models of preventive medicine, holistic health and stress management have permeated the mainstream of western medicine.

In 1989 Swamiji returned to India where he established the Himalayan Institute Hospital Trust in the foothills of the Garhwal Himalayas. Swamiji left this physical plane in November 1996, but the seeds he has sown continue to sprout, bloom, and bear fruit. His teachings embodied in the words 'Love, Serve, Remember' continue to inspire the many students whose good fortune it was to come in contact with such an accomplished, selfless, and loving master.

Himalayan Institute Hospital Trust

The Himalayan Institute Hospital Trust (HIHT) was conceived, designed, and orchestrated by Dr. Swami Rama, a yogi, scientist, researcher, writer, and humanitarian. The mission of HIHT is to develop integrated and cost-effective approaches to health care and development for the country as a whole, and for under-served populations worldwide.

Swamiji started this project in 1989 with an outpatient clinic of only two rooms. The hospital at HIHT currently has 750 beds and is serving approximately 10 million people of Garhwal, Kumaon and adjoining areas. The hospital includes a Reference Laboratory, Emergency Wing, Operation Theaters, Blood Bank, Eye Bank, Dialysis Unit, I.C.U., C.C.U., Cath Lab., and a state-of-the-art Radiology Department. The newly established Cancer Research Institute is providing radiation therapy in addition to chemotherapy and surgical oncology.

The Rural Development Institute is providing healthcare, education, income generation opportunities, water and sanitation programs, adolescent awareness programs and other quality of life improvement programs in the villages of Uttarakhand and adjoining rural areas.

The Himalayan Institute of Medical Sciences has now become HIHT University, a deemed university, recognized by the University Grants Commission. The University runs undergraduate (M.B.B.S.) and postgraduate courses (M.D./ M.S. and Diploma) in 15 disciplines. The medical faculty is also conducting paramedical degree courses in Medical Laboratory Technology, Radiology & Imaging Technology, and Physiotherapy.

The Himalayan College of Nursing offers a four-year B.Sc. program and a 3-year GNM diploma program. The uniqueness of these nursing programs is that the nursing students are provided hands-on training in the community and with the rural population.

In keeping with Swamiji's mission of integration, the hospital runs outpatient Ayurveda and Homeopathy clinics and the Ayurveda Center provides a residential Panchakarma therapy program for detoxification, rejuvenation and treatment of chronic ailments. The Combined Therapy Program, pioneered by Swami Rama, has been a unique model of holistic health care for more than 30 years. The Combined Therapy Program combines biofeedback, hatha yoga, aerobic exercise, nutrition, breathing, relaxation skills, meditation and other self-awareness techniques.

For information contact:

Himalayan Institute Hospital Trust
Swami Ram Nagar
P.O. Doiwala, Distt. Dehradun 248140
Uttarakhand, India
91-135-247-1200
pb@hihtindia.org
www.hihtindia.org

Swami Rama Society, Inc.

The Swami Rama Society is a registered, nonprofit, tax-exempt organization committed to Swami Rama's vision of bridging the gap between Western science and Eastern wisdom through the integration of body, mind, and spirit. The Society was established to provide financial assistance and technical support to institutions and individuals who are ready to implement this vision in the U.S.A. and abroad.

For information contact:

Swami Rama Society, Inc.
5000 W Vliet St.
Milwaukee, WI 53211 U.S.A.
414-273-1621
info@swamiramasociety.org
www.swamiramasociety.org

At the Feet of a Himalayan Master

Remembering Swami Rama
Volume One
ISBN 978-81-88157-62-4,Rs. 250,
paperback, 344 pages

At the Feet of a Himalayan Master

Remembering Swami Rama
Volume Two
ISBN 978-81-88157-66-2, Rs. 240,
paperback, 304 pages

Conscious Living

*A Guidebook for Spiritual
Transformation*
Swami Rama
ISBN 978-188157-03-7, Rs. 120,
paperback, 160 pages

Let the Bud of Life Bloom

*A Guide to Raising Happy and Healthy
Children*
Swami Rama
ISBN 978-188157-04-4, Rs. 120,
paperback, 102 pages

Distributed in India by Swami Rama Centre,
Himalayan Institute Hospital Trust, Jolly Grant,
PO Doiwala, Dehradun 248140, Uttarakhand,
India, src@hihtindia.org, 135-241-2068

Samadhi the Highest State of Wisdom
Yoga the Sacred Science, volume one
Swami Rama
ISBN 978-81-88157-01-3, Rs. 175, paperback, 256 pages

Sadhana the Path to Enlightenment
Yoga the Sacred Science, volume two
Swami Rama
ISBN 978-81-88157-68-6, Rs. 240, paperback, 310 pages

OM the Eternal Witness
Secrets of the Mandukya Upanishad
Swami Rama
ISBN 978-81-88157-43-3, Rs. 150, paperback, 202 pages

Sacred Journey
Living Purposefully and Dying Gracefully
Swami Rama
ISBN 978-81-88157-00-6, Rs. 75, paperback, 136 pages

Distributed in India by Swami Rama Centre, Himalayan Institute Hospital Trust, Jolly Grant, PO Doiwala, Dehradun 248140, Uttarakhand, India, src@hihtindia.org, 135-241-2068